When
FOOTBALL *Was*
FOOTBALL

TOTTENHAM HOTSPUR

A Nostalgic Look at a Century of the Club

First published in 2009

A catalogue record for this book is available from the British Library

ISBN: 978-1-844259-48-9

Published by Haynes Publishing, Sparkford, Yeovil,
Somerset BA22 7JJ, UK
Tel: 01963 442030 Fax: 01963 440001
Int. tel: +44 1963 442030 Int. fax: +44 1963 440001
E-mail: sales@haynes.co.uk
Website: www.haynes.co.uk

Haynes North America Inc., 861 Lawrence Drive,
Newbury Park, California 91320, USA

All images © Mirrorpix

Creative Director: Kevin Gardner
Design and Artwork: David Wildish
Packaged for Haynes by Green Umbrella Publishing

Printed and bound in Britain by J F Print Ltd., Sparkford, Somerset

When
FOOTBALL *Was* FOOTBALL

TOTTENHAM HOTSPUR

A Nostalgic Look at a Century of the Club

Adam Powley

Foreword by Steve Perryman

Contents

Foreword

Footballers and managers are often heard to say that they ignore the newspapers. "Tomorrow's chip paper" is the usual comment, but the truth is we all read them. When I first became a regular in the Spurs team back in 1969, the *Daily Mirror* was my paper, and down the years I used to read the match reports of great reporters like Frank McGhee, Ken Montgomery and Harry Miller. They were good old-fashioned journos who knew their football and merited respect – even if I didn't always agree with some of the opinions they expressed!

Through almost all of Tottenham's rich history, the *Mirror* and its sister papers have been there to report on the great games, the famous players, the cup-winning successes, and the heartbreaks as well. The photographs in this book make those events and characters come alive: famous victories in the FA Cup, the epic Double season, the unforgettable glory, glory nights in Europe, and legendary players like Ron Burgess, Dave Mackay, Danny Blanchflower, Jimmy Greaves, Glenn Hoddle, Ossie Ardiles, and, of course, Mr Tottenham himself, the late, great Bill Nicholson.

I am immensely proud and privileged to hold the record for the highest number of appearances for Spurs, with over 850 games under my belt. It was a real honour to be captain for so many of them, and looking at these evocative photos brings back some much-cherished memories.

The pictures also serve as a reminder that there's something special and unique about Tottenham Hotspur. Even if the club hasn't been as successful as it perhaps should have been in recent years, it's still one of the best-supported and most famous clubs in the world. This is a celebration of a golden age for football, and a fine portrait of a wonderful club.

Steve Perryman

The Flower of the South
1900-1949

Jimmy Dimmock (right foreground in the white shirt near the corner of the six-yard box) scores the goal that beat Wolves 1-0 at a rain-drenched Stamford Bridge in 1921, securing Tottenham's second FA Cup triumph.

> ❝
> *The Spurs will play fast, clever football of the First League type.*
> Daily Mirror correspondent
> P J Moss, 1921
> ❞

1900 Tottenham Hotspur win the Southern League championship, earning the nickname "Flower of the South" 1901 Nineteen years after the club's formation, Spurs win the FA Cup, becoming the only non-league side ever to do so 1908 Tottenham join the Football League, winning promotion to Division One at the first attempt 1909 Walter Tull becomes the first black player to appear for the club and the first black outfield player in English football 1910 First league win over Arsenal, 3-1 at White Hart Lane 1913 Peter McWilliam becomes manager, taking over team responsibilities from the board 1914 First World War begins, White Hart Lane converted into a gas mask factory 1919 Arsenal steal Tottenham's place in Division One after a hugely controversial vote taken at an infamous meeting to choose sides for the expanded Football League 1920 Spurs regain top-flight status with a record 70 points 1921 Tottenham win FA Cup for second time 1922 League runners-up, then-highest placing by a London team 1928 Relegated to Division Two in the "freak" season in which just seven points separated the fourth and bottom sides 1933 Promoted back to Division One, relegated just two seasons later 1934 Opening of new East Stand, home of the famous Shelf 1938 Record home attendance: 75,038 v Sunderland, FA Cup fifth round; Bill Nicholson signs for the club 1939-45 Wartime football; the East Stand used as a temporary morgue for victims of the Blitz 1949 Arthur Rowe appointed manager

ve been
eat him
sion ran
Hastings
Steeple-
and the
pswich,
coff, a
unners.

e pace
and it
rs, but
w with
Baton
or 110

made
s, who
ed an
, and
in at
ged to
Percy
their
was

Hib-
gnifi-
gall,
post,
ceed-
urite

lling
iner,
the
both
com-
uin.

three lengths; two lengths between second and third.

TO-DAY'S PROGRAMME.

2.0—MAIDEN HURDLE RACE of 100 sovs. Two miles.

HORST PARK

	yrs st lb		yrs st lb
Happy Slave	6 11 7	Barnstormer	4 10 7
Liza Johnson	5 11 3	a Melayr	4 10 7
a Jason		Kava	4 10 7
The Chair	6 11 3	Chapeau	4 10 7
General Cronje	5 11 3	Henley	4 10 7
Jollybird	5 11 3	Plinlimmon	4 10 7
Red Orchid	4 10 7		

YESTERDAY'S CUP-TIE—TOTTENHAM v. MIDDLESBROUGH.

A brilliant save by Williamson (Middlesbrough's goalkeeper) from Bull, Tottenham's great centre half-back, at yesterday's replayed Cup-tie at Tottenham.—
("Daily Mirror" copyright.)

2.30—GARRETT MOORE HANDICAP STEEPLE-CHASE of 300 sovs. Two miles.

	yrs st lb		yrs st lb
Drumree	a 12 7	The Clown II	5 10 12
The Actuary	a 12 4	Dathi	a 10 11
Phil May	6 11 12	Commondale	6 10 10
a St. Moritz	a 11 12	Azro	a 10 9
Key West	a 11 11	Amethyst	6 10 6
Shylock II.	5 11 9	a Kepler	5 10 5
Buckhunter	a 11 5	Developer	5 10 0
Eva	6 11 3	Royal Rouge	a 10 0
Grand Deacon	a 11 1	Lady Malta	6 10 0
Communist	a 11 0	Fair Geraldine	4 10 0
Æsthetic Anne	a 10 12		

3.0—TEDDINGTON SELLING HURDLE RACE of 100 sovs; winner to be sold for 50 sovs. Two miles.

	yrs st lb		yrs st lb
a A.N.B.	a 11 7	a Queen of the Bees	5 11 7
a Preen	6 11 7	a Wimpole	a 10 7
a Maori Queen II	a 11 7	a Cypka	4 10 7
a Revera	a 11 7	a Wild Gander	4 10 7
a Royal Blaze	a 11 7	a Emu	4 10 7
a Masquerade	5 11 3	a Honore	4 10 7
a Oasis	a 11 7	a Ohlora	4 10 7
a Free Breeze	5 11 3	a Malverley	4 10 7

3.30—OVERNIGHT SELLING STEEPLECHASE

John Cameron told me on Monday that Williamson, the Middlesbrough keeper, prevented the 'Spurs from winning last Saturday. And yesterday Williamson again had the angels on his side. His form in goal savoured of the miraculous, and the point against came from a long, raking corner kick by Walton.

Tottenham's friends must have had their hearts in their mouths in the first few minutes. Eggett nearly fumbled several things; but the trusty Tait was always about in the nick of time. But here was Bell missing an open goal—a breathless escape for the 'Spurs.

* * *

But in five minutes the 'Spurs found their game, and then literally there was only "one side in it." The

Middlesbrough forwards were virtually outclassed. But their full-backs and their halves played with unflagging energy. Of course, Vivian Woodward was well marked; but he played beautiful football; his dribbling with either foot was continually outwitting the defence as he swung out the ball to Walton.

Everyone of the 'Spurs played to Walton's wing, and the brilliant, fair-headed forward was completely worthy of the attention bestowed on him. His pace, his dribbling, his centres were alike wonderful, and the "old parliamentary hand" came strongly in evidence as he crossed inside to get the return pass from Woodward.

* * *

Glen was not on one of his best days. He did a lot of fair work, and was clever with his feet, but he was slow, and was always disclosing his tactics before putting them to the test.

* * *

Kirwan had not much to do, but O'Hagan put in a rare lot of brilliant work, although rather giver much finesse

competition.

FINE RUNN

In the two mile College sports, (Caius), the thr from scratch in which beats his p

He took the lea beat A. R. Wel A. S. D. Smith holder, ran third

YESTI

R
This match of I
Hall yesterday.
In the afternoon
238 (unfinished).
Roberts only adde
evening. His othe
made runs of 110
(receives 5,500), 15

IN
Inman and Taylo
at the Soho-square
an unfinished 207 to
and 61. Taylor's b
(receives 2,000), 5,10

Stock Market
—Kaffir Ma
Ra

CAPEL COURT, Th
kets were in gallopin
perhaps not quite so
evening, but then it
ment for one thing,
business. Investment
tone of the markets w
of bad news, and th
expected death of M
the Chartered Compan
evening at Sidmouth.
Day, but the later ne
fact, he was expected b
news affected Chartere
desians as a whole v
Kaffirs were not so
trust did not arouse
yesterday. In other m
to find anything to no
Egyptians were firmer.
The Bank rate showed
a very strong one and

9

The Daily Mirror Reports on Tottenham Hotspur

Veteran of the 1901 cup-winning side, Alexander Tait was one of a number of Scotsmen who starred for Tottenham in the 1900s. Hailing from Glenbuck, the same Ayrshire village as team-mate Sandy Brown, Tait played over 400 games for the club.

A. Tait, of Tottenham Hotspur.—(Purdie.)

TRAINING AT TOTTENHAM FOR THE FOOTBALL SEASON.

Though the cricketing season is still at its height footballers are not allowing the grass to grow under their feet. Already the first-class clubs are preparing strenuously for the football season, which will start almost before cricketers have had time to pull their stumps out of the ground. 1 and 2 show members of the Tottenham Hotspur Club engaged in running and wrestling exercises

MISCELLANEOUS SPORT.

The match between the M.C.C. team and Eighteen of Bendigo had to be abandoned yesterday on account of heavy rain. The following were the scores at the close of play:—Eighteen of Bendigo: First innings, 94; second innings, 64 for seven wickets. M.C.C.: First innings, 273 for five wickets (innings declared closed).

Yesterday, under Association football rules, the following First Division League matches were played:—Wolverhampton Wanderers beat Liverpool at Wolverhampton by 4 goals to 2; West Bromwich Albion beat Blackburn Rovers at West Bromwich by 2 goals to 0; Sheffield United, at Sheffield, beat Manchester City by 5 goals to 3; Derby County drew with Aston Villa, 2 goals each, at Derby; and Stoke drew pointless with Middlesborough at Stoke.

The following were Southern League results:—Portsmouth v. Plymouth Argyle, a draw—no scoring; West Ham 2, Fulham 0; Reading 2, Brighton and Hove 2; Millwall 3, Brentford 1; Bristol Rovers 7, Wellingborough 1; Northampton 2, Queen's Park Rangers 1; Luton 2, Kettering 1; New Brompton 3, Swindon 1.

In the Western League Tottenham Hotspur beat Southampton (1—0), and amongst results in other matches were: Corinthians 5, Notts County 3; Oxford City 1, Casuals 1.

There were one or two interesting Rugby matches yesterday. Bedford entertained the Racing Club de France, and won unexpectedly easily by 44 points to nil; Cardiff beat Old Merchant Taylors at Cardiff by 13 points to nil; Newport, at Newport, beat the Barbarians by 17 points to 5; Leicester, at home, beat Cheltenham by 21 points to 0; Exeter beat Belfast Collegians, at Exeter, by 18 points to 0; and Bristol beat Coventry, at Bristol, by 26 points to 8.

Above: The first surviving mention of Tottenham Hotspur in the pages of the *Daily Mirror*, on Tuesday 29th December 1903 – a brief acknowledgement of a 1-0 victory against Southampton in the Western League, beneath the underwhelming heading of "Miscellaneous Sport".

Left: Football's – and Tottenham's – increasing popularity was reflected in reports on close-season training, even in the midst of the cricket season.

A section of the enormous crowd at Tottenham cheering after the home team's second goal. It is estimated that 35,000 people were present.

MISS EDNA MAY PRESENTS PRIZES AT FOOTBALL MATCH

Yesterday Tottenham Hotspur and Southampton met at Tottenham in the final for the Southern Charity Cup, given by the "Evening News." The photograph shows Miss Edna May making a speech after presenting the Cup and medals to the Tottenham team, who were victorious by 2 goals to nil.—("Daily Mirror" photograph.)

Above: Even as early as the 1900s, Spurs had a reputation for attracting a "showbiz" crowd. For this Southern Charity Cup final victory over Southampton in 1907, the great American actress and singing star Miss Edna May was in attendance and on hand to award the trophy.

Below: The FA Cup held a more "newsworthy" appeal in the Edwardian era than league games. The *Mirror* devoted generous coverage to a 7-1 thrashing of Plymouth in January 1910.

TOTTENHAM HOTSPUR BEAT PLYMOUTH ARGYLE BY 7 GOALS TO 1 AT WHITE HART LANE.

Taking full advantage of the fact that they were playing at home, Tottenham Hotspur yesterday defeated Plymouth Argyle in a replayed English Cup-tie by 7 goals to 1. In the first match, played at Plymouth on Saturday, the game resulted in a draw of one goal all.

(1) Headwork—Plymouth are in the dark jerseys. (2) An exciting moment in front of the Argyle's goal. (3) The Argyle's goalkeeper saving. (4) Tottenham man claiming a foul.—(*Daily Mirror*, Half-Tones, and L.N.A.)

By the time the *Daily Mirror* was up and running in late 1903, Tottenham Hotspur were arguably one of the biggest clubs in the country – certainly of the region. The professional game and the Football League were still dominated by Northern and Midlands sides, but, having won the FA Cup as a non-league team in 1901, Spurs had become nationally famous and had a support to match. Key to the club's appeal was its commitment to entertaining, attacking football that drew huge crowds to White Hart Lane – twice in the 1903-04 Cup run, home games were abandoned due to supporters spilling onto the pitch to escape pressure in the packed stands.

It was a reflection on how football was cementing its position as the leading mass spectator sport, and Spurs enjoyed a boom in popularity. For the 3-1 win over Sheffield Wednesday in September 1910, the *Mirror* estimated the crowd at 35,000, though the recorded attendance was given as 29,200. Here (far bottom left) amid a special photographic feature on the weekend's football action, jubilant home supporters celebrate Bobby Steel's goal.

Competitive football continued well into the First World War, until public and official mood prompted a suspension of the league. White Hart Lane played its part in the war effort. The stands were converted into workshops making gas masks and other protective equipment, while the pitch was turned over for military drill practice.

These rather sobering pictures from 1916 show some of the workshop staff wearing leather hoods with eyeholes cut out, while colleagues at their benches halt production for a moment to pose for the camera. Virtually all the workers were female.

The FA Cup 1921

In 1921 Tottenham earned their second major trophy with a 1-0 win over Wolves. The triumph was just reward for the dedication of manager Peter McWilliam and his talented group of players, and went some way to making up for the club's controversial relegation from Division One in 1919 at the hands of Arsenal chairman, Henry Norris, who engineered the election that promoted his club at Tottenham's expense.

Skippered by the elegant half-back and later England captain Arthur Grimsdell, who gave almost 18 years to the Tottenham cause, the Spurs team carried all before them in a record-breaking promotion campaign in 1919/20. Two years later the side finished as runners-up to Liverpool in the League Championship. Arsenal, by then firmly established as Tottenham's bitterest rivals after their move from south London to Highbury, finished sixth from bottom.

Above: The victorious Spurs squad proudly displaying their 1921 trophy haul. The Charity Shield was secured with a 2-0 win against league champions Burnley. Captain Arthur Grimsdell is seated immediately to the left of the FA Cup.

Left: Amid stories of society weddings and scandalous court cases, the FA Cup final was big news. The preview for the 1921 game argued that "no previous cup final has aroused greater public interest".

–LEGENDS–

Jimmy Dimmock

A common observation on football then and now is that the stars of yesteryear did not enjoy anything like the financial rewards lesser modern players have been able to reap. The story of Jimmy Dimmock is a telling illustration of that point.

Born in Edmonton, Dimmock was the only Londoner in Tottenham's 1921 FA Cup final side, scored the winning goal and went on to carve out a Spurs career that made him one of the club's true greats. A dazzling winger with outstanding close control, he made 438 senior appearances, scored 100 league goals, won England caps and was regarded as one of the superstars of his era. Yet by the Thirties, along with millions of others he was unemployed and his family faced grinding poverty amid the Great Depression. In an age of maximum wages when players were regarded virtually as servants by clubs, a professional footballer was vulnerable as almost anyone to economic hardship, especially after they retired from the game without a trade to fall back on. In March 1934, the Mirror reported that Dimmock, his wife and five children were facing eviction for rent arrears from their Edmonton home. Fortunately his old club stepped in to settle the bill.

FOOTBALL –STATS–

Jimmy Dimmock

Name: James Henry Dimmock

Born: 1900

Died: 1972

Playing Career: 1919-1931

Clubs: Tottenham Hotspur, Thames, Clapton Orient

Tottenham Appearances: 438

Goals: 112

Above: Even in the 1920s, golf and football were happy partners. In April 1924, the *Mirror* organized a special golf contest between teams from the capital. Spurs entered three sides, pitted against teams from Arsenal, Fulham and individual players from other clubs.

Spurs players pictured are: Frank Osborne (second left), Bert Smith (third left), Charlie Walters (second right) and Billy Sage (first right).

Left: In happier circumstances, Dimmock was pictured in the *Sunday People* in May 1962, sitting at home watching his old club win the FA Cup on television.

17

The Pre-War Blues

The FA Cup tended to provide Tottenham's brighter moments. Here Jack Gibbons scores for Spurs in a 5-2, fourth round replay win over New Brighton in 1938.

The 1930s was to be Tottenham's most unsuccessful decade. It began with Spurs recording their lowest ever league position (finishing 12th in Division Two) and the club played only two seasons in the top flight. Spurs were still buoyant, however: Percy Smith's "Greyhounds" side maintained Tottenham's reputation for fast attacking football at the beginning of the 1930s, crowds held up, White Hart Lane continued to take impressive shape with the completion of the magnificent East Stand, and despite the long period of economic decline, finances were robust – Tottenham recorded a profit of nearly £9,000 for the 1934/35 season.

Bert Sproston closes in on Arsenal's Bryn Jones during the Jubilee Trust meeting between the north London rivals in August 1938. The game was held as part of the league's 50th anniversary, one of several derby games organized to raise contributions for the league's benevolent fund, which was set up to help players who "may have fallen into distress". Spurs won 2-0.

November 1938 and Spurs parade the man who would become the greatest signing ever made by the club. Not Fred Sargent (left), a stalwart through the 1930s and war years who made nearly 100 appearances for the club, but one William Edward Nicholson. He had signed from Northfleet (Tottenham's nursery side) three months earlier, went on to play over 300 games and as manager turned Spurs into the best side in the country.

For a club that has a long tradition of drawing significant support from London's Jewish community, the sight of German players and fans giving Nazi salutes at White Hart Lane still causes shock over 70 years after the event.

The Spurs stadium was the venue for an international match on 4th December 1935 between England and Germany, won 3-0 by the hosts. Around 12,000 German fans – many were believed to be members of the "Strength Through Joy" Nazi sport movement – made the trip, taking advantage of cheap boat-train fares. There were even subsequent rumours that the visitors used the trip to reconnoitre London's streets in readiness for future bombing by the Luftwaffe. Arriving at Spurs, the German fans massed on the lower tier of the East Stand.

Despite calls from left-wing parties and Jewish groups for the game to be cancelled, and an official delegation from the TUC meeting Home Secretary Sir John Simon to voice their fears, the match went ahead – though one supporter made his own personal stand. Earnest Wooley was arrested for cutting down the German flag at the ground, but had his case dismissed.

With normal competitive football largely placed on hold during the Second World War, Tottenham Hotspur emerged in the latter half of the 1940s seeking to re-establish the club as one of the biggest in the country. With players such as Len Duquemin, Eddie Baily, Les Bennett, Sonny Walters and Alf Ramsey added to the fold and making their debuts in the latter half of the decade, the personnel were in place for Tottenham's next great side.

Spurs keeper Ted Ditchburn (right) exchanges pleasantries with his Arsenal counterpart George Swindin just before their meeting in the FA Cup in January 1949. Cliff Lloyd, Fulham defender and later PFA secretary, keeps the peace.

White Hart Lane thankfully emerged relatively unscathed from the Blitz, unlike much of the surrounding area. With a capacity of almost 80,000, it was an ideal venue for big matches, as shown here with action from England's 2-0 defeat of Italy in November 1949.

Len Duquemin (right) challenges for the ball during Tottenham's 2-0 win over Cardiff in December 1949. The victory helped Spurs towards the Division Two title, and they finished a full nine points ahead of their nearest challengers, Sheffield Wednesday. Spurs

Push and Run
1950-1959

> *Make it simple, make it accurate, make it quick.*
> Arthur Rowe

Arthur Rowe: Tottenham fan, player, title-winning manager, visionary.

1949-50 Arthur Rowe appointed manager; completes his first season as Tottenham boss, winning promotion with a new style of pass and movement dubbed "Push and Run" **1950** Spurs thrash Newcastle – Jackie Milburn and all – 7-0, proving that the tactic could be mercilessly successful in the top flight **1951** Tottenham beat Sheffield Wednesday 1-0 at White Hart Lane to become champions for the first time **1952** Spurs finish as runners-up to Manchester United **1953** Defeat to Blackpool in FA Cup semi-final five years after losing to the same side at the same stage **1954** Danny Blanchflower signs for £30,000 **1955** Rowe retires due to ill health; former groundstaff member, player, trainer, coach and assistant manager Jimmy Anderson takes over **1956** Spurs avoid relegation by just two points **1957** The West Stand cockerel and ball statue is moved to the East Stand to enable an upgrade of the floodlights **1958** Bill Nicholson becomes manager **1959** Dave Mackay signs from Hearts for a record £32,000

Practice makes perfect... The fundamentals of "Push and Run" were carefully honed on the training ground and on the hard courts tucked away at the back of White Hart Lane. With talents such as Len Duquemin (second right) and Ron Burgess (right) at his disposal, Rowe's revolutionary system proved devastatingly successful.

–LEGENDS–

Ron Burgess

Like many of his South Wales compatriots, football provided Ron Burgess with an escape route away from a lifetime of work down the pits. The game, and Spurs in particular, should be thankful such a true great was able to express himself on the football pitch.

Burgess survived initial doubts about his future at Tottenham, in no small part thanks to an impressive performance in a trial match that he was chosen to play in at the last minute, just as he was about to return to Wales. He soon became the "next big thing" at the club before war intervened. On being made captain of the team, he operated as Rowe's on-field lieutenant, tactician and prime exponent, blessed with supreme skill to match a ceaseless work rate. The manager's bold philosophy hinged on picking players with excellent technical ability who were able to control, pass and move at speed. Burgess made the Push-and-Run ideal a reality.

FOOTBALL
–STATS–

Ron Burgess

Name: William Arthur Ronald Burgess

Born: 1917

Died: 2005

Playing Career: 1938-1958

Clubs: Tottenham Hotspur, Swansea

Tottenham Appearances: 328

Goals: 17

> "The perfect footballer
> *Bill Nicholson, on Ron Burgess*"

29

> *Football's a simple game, it's the players who make it difficult.*
>
> Arthur Rowe

The Push-and-Run side were packed with talent from front to back. Steeped in Tottenham traditions of fluent football and inspired by Rowe's groundbreaking philosophy, some among this band of talented brothers replicated the team's success as managers. Bill Nicholson and Alf Ramsey both went on to win the league title as bosses, Ramsey, of course, won the World Cup, and Eddie Baily proved an able right-hand man to Nicholson.

Left: Ramsey was first identified as a potential Spurs player by Rowe's predecessor, Joe Hulme (who deserves much credit for the legacy of talent he bequeathed to his successor). As the embodiment of the "ball-playing full-back" Ramsey slotted effortlessly into the Spurs side, becoming one of the most important cogs within this supremely efficient machine. Here he is in typically assured action during the famous 7-0 mauling of Newcastle in November 1950.

Above: Inside-left Les Medley, another home-grown lad from Edmonton, was the dashing foil to Eddie Baily's prompting.

e Push-and-Run side scored fun, but without a dependable n between the posts, all the e attacking work would have nted for little. Whether in the at of a game, or even, as below, he 1951 Christmas Party, Ted tchburn proved to be more than able of the role. An England ernational, Ditchburn provided years of loyal service and set cord for consecutive club pearances – 247 between 1948 d 1954.

Life at White Hart Lane

The East Stand, looking resplendent in the summer sunshine, provides a packed backdrop to Leslie Dicker's attempt to beat a prostrate Norman Heath, West Brom's goalkeeper. A crowd of 56,552 was on hand to see Spurs go down to a surprise 4-3 defeat in August 1952.

"You've never had it so good" trumpeted Prime Minister Harold Macmillan in 1957. For a couple of years at the beginning of the decade, Tottenham Hotspur's fortunes never appeared so bright. The title-winning season proved to be a short-lived success, as an ageing team declined and Rowe's poor health caused by the stress of the job led to his resignation in 1955. But White Hart

EDDIE BAILY, sharp-shooting forward for Tottenham Hotspur, is well on the way to high football honours. A natural forcing player, famed for his ball-control, Eddie has already represented England twice this season — against Switzerland and Austria — and turns out regularly for the Football League. Like many top athletes, Eddie smokes Craven 'A'. "Because," he says, "they're never *rough*.".

"The one cigarette I really like..."

SAYS 'SPURS STAR *Eddie Baily*

"YOU'D BE SURPRISED," says Eddie Baily, "how dry your mouth feels after a big match. That's why I stay with Craven 'A'— whenever I light one up, the flavour of the tobacco comes through mellow and satisfying, just the way I want it. I couldn't *afford* to smoke a cigarette that irritated my throat. . . ."

Craven 'A' for smooth, clean Smoking

P.S. That cork tip really does make a difference, you know. There's a lot more pleasure in a cigarette with an end that's always clean, and dry, and firm between your lips.

Above: North London rivalry was put to one side when Arsenal commissioned a special statuette by the acclaimed artist and sculptor Benno Elkan. The cockerel artwork was presented to Spurs in December 1950.

Right: From the start of the professional game, advertisers had been keen to associate products with footballers. In an age long before macro-diets and a more responsible understanding of the dangers of smoking, Eddie Baily lent his name to "Craven A" cigarettes because "they are never rough".

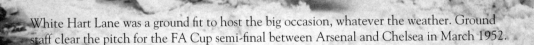

White Hart Lane was a ground fit to host the big occasion, whatever the weather. Ground staff clear the pitch for the FA Cup semi-final between Arsenal and Chelsea in March 1952.

33

White Hart Lane had its share of passionate and colourful characters on the terraces and in the stands, as this happy pair demonstrates in January 1954.

Hackney-born Tommy "the Charmer" Harmer was one of the most popular players of the 1950s at Tottenham. The club repeatedly tried to build up his physique – he was just 5ft 6in and barely 8½ stone dripping wet – as seen in this weight-training session from October 1952. It was to no avail, but no matter – Harmer went on to make over 200 appearances for Spurs, scoring 51 goals.

Scorer of the title-winning goal against Sheffield Wednesday in 1951, Len "The Duke" Duquemin was not the most elegant player in the Push-and-Run team, but his wholehearted bravery made the Channel Islander hugely popular with team-mates and on the terraces. Here he is in typically committed action in the 4-0 defeat of Blackpool on 18th October 1952.

Left: White Hart Lane had its sombre moments. Two days after the death of King George VI, the Spurs and Arsenal teams line up for a minute's silence: 9th February 1952.

Right: "Two together?" Ticket touting is almost as old as the game itself, and White Hart Lane had long been a lucrative venue for those with "spares". For the FA Cup semi-final match between Luton and Norwich staged at the ground in March 1959, one enterprising trader does brisk business.

Far Left: For all the glamour and fame of being an elite footballer in the 1950s, the financial rewards were still modest. Wages were better than average, but the maximum salary of £20 per week in 1958 exceeded that of the "man in the street" by only £5. Small wonder that many players, Ted Ditchburn among them, supplemented their football earnings with other sources of income. Here he is in 1957, pictured in his grocer's shop not far from White Hart Lane. Ditchburn was something of an entrepreneur. He had also owned a theatre and coach ticket agency in nearby Northumberland Park and later ran an electrical retailer, a toy shop, and a sports shop in Romford.

Below Left: Jimmy Anderson took over managerial duties from Rowe in 1955. Though he only lasted three full seasons, he proved to be a vital link between the Push-and-Run era and the emerging Double side, taking Spurs to a league runners-up spot behind the Busby Babes in 1957 and an FA Cup semi-final the year before. On the eve of that game against Manchester City, Anderson briefs Duquemin in training.

Top Left: In a portent of things to come, Bill Nicholson passes on his wisdom to one of Anderson's best signings, Bobby Smith. Nicholson had acted as first-team coach for three years before his promotion to manager.

Below: Another of Anderson's shrewdly purchased recruits, Maurice Norman (far right), trains with team-mates. Note the heavy, old, leather-panelled footballs: the design of the most fundamental object in the game had barely altered from its 19th-century original, and synthetic waterproof balls started to appear only in the 1960s.

The Path to Glory

The seeds of the Double side's success were sown well before Bill Nicholson became manager on 11th October 1958. The style and panache in the way the team played was a fundamental part of the club's tradition, while many of the key players were already at Spurs having been signed or come through the ranks. Though he was not to feature in the 1960/61 season, Tommy Harmer, pictured here in training at Cheshunt, had a key role in the evolution of Nicholson's team. He scored with a thunderous half-volley in Tottenham's 10-4 demolition of Everton, Nicholson's first game in charge. Danny Blanchflower, with typical wit, cautioned his boss that "it's all downhill from here". He couldn't have been further from the truth.

> *We don't score 10 every week, you know*
> **Tommy Harmer**

Left: Nicholson placed an emphasis on team spirit among a relatively small core of players (only 17 were used during the Double season). From a 1959 dressing room team photo, in the midst of old hands like Harmer, new faces like Dave Mackay (fourth from left behind Maurice Norman) began to make their presence felt.

Below Left: Gathered around the radio listening to the FA Cup draw in February 1959, Cliff Jones leans on skipper Danny Blanchflower and Johnny Brooks. Brooks's place up front was later to be taken by John White.

> *Nicholson's system had individual expression but it was based on teamwork.*
> Walter Winterbottom, England manager

Spurs struggled in Nicholson's first season and finished fifth from bottom. Playing on mud-heap pitches in midwinter may not have helped Tottenham's silky style but Manchester United had no problem adjusting to the conditions, running out 3-1 winners at White Hart Lane in February 1959. Despite being extensively upgraded in 1953, when 3,500 tons of soil were dug up and dumped on Hackney Marshes, the Spurs surface still proved difficult to maintain.

Hoisted aloft by Bobby Smith (left) and Maurice Norman, Danny Blanchflower proudly lifts the FA Cup in 1962.

Blanchflower is pictured with Jimmy Anderson leaving a memorial service for the victims of the Munich Air Disaster at London's St Martin in the Fields church, February 1958. A deep thinker with a passion for the finer qualities of football, Blanchflower was a natural communicator and a media favourite who later became a distinguished journalist, but he had no time for petty celebrity. He famously became the first person to turn down an invitation from Eammon Andrews to appear as the subject of *This Is Your Life*. "I consider this programme to be an invasion of privacy," he said. "Nobody is going to press-gang me into anything."

> *An original piece of artwork.*
> Hunter Davis on Danny Blanchflower

–LEGENDS–

Danny Blanchflower

He was not a prolific goalscorer, his tackling was competent but hardly earth-shattering, and he was supposedly past his prime when Spurs began the 1960s with hopes of winning a second league title. But in every other respect, Danny Blanchflower was world class.

Widely regarded as Tottenham's greatest ever player, Blanchflower had no equal when it came to dictating a game of football on the field. His supreme control, magnificent passing ability and reading of the game made him stand out out as a genuine superstar, but it was his knack for translating that almost instinctive expertise to the benefit of his team-mates that made him special. He was the definition of an inspirational captain, the commanding genius who put Nicholson's ideas and strategies into lethal, beautiful practice.

Twice Footballer of the Year, off the pitch he was intelligent, mischievous, fascinating, witty and wise, a larger-than-life, opinionated character who was no respecter of position or privilege. These traits frequently put him at odds with authority, which only served to make him even more of a hero to his many admirers, Spurs fans or otherwise. He was a one-off; there simply will never be another Danny Blanchflower.

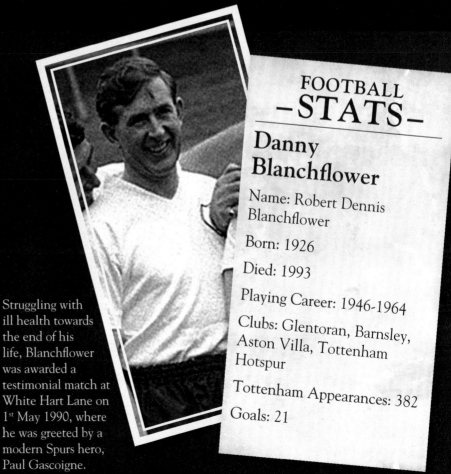

Struggling with ill health towards the end of his life, Blanchflower was awarded a testimonial match at White Hart Lane on 1st May 1990, where he was greeted by a modern Spurs hero, Paul Gascoigne.

FOOTBALL –STATS–

Danny Blanchflower

Name: Robert Dennis Blanchflower

Born: 1926

Died: 1993

Playing Career: 1946-1964

Clubs: Glentoran, Barnsley, Aston Villa, Tottenham Hotspur

Tottenham Appearances: 382

Goals: 21

Left: In common with other clubs, a train engine had been named in Tottenham's honour. Previously known as "Thoresby Park" until it was renamed "Tottenham Hotspur" in 1938, it was a B17 locomotive that had worked the LNER line until withdrawn from service in 1958. The nameplate was transferred to the entrance to the dressing rooms at White Hart Lane. B17 No 2830 may have come to a halt but by 1960 when this picture was taken, the Spurs express was unstoppable.

Below: By the time the new decade arrived, Nicholson's team were starting to hit their stride, as Bobby Smith slid in to score his and Tottenham's second in a 2-1 defeat of Manchester United on 23rd January 1960. Spurs finished third that season, but they were just warming up.

The Double
1960-1961

> *Mind you, football is not really about winning, or goals, or saves or supporters. It's about glory. It's about doing things in style, doing them with a flourish. It's about going out to beat the other lot, not waiting for them to die of boredom. It's about dreaming of the glory of the Double.*
>
> Danny Blanchflower

Standing on the cusp of greatness . . . In March 1961, poised to win the League Championship, and readying themselves for a final assault on the FA Cup, the famous Spurs team that passed into football immortality. Left to right: Cliff Jones, John White, Danny Blanchflower, Maurice Norman, Peter Baker, Bill Brown, Ron Henry, Dave Mackay, Les Allen, Bobby Smith, Terry Dyson.

It is almost half a century since millions of football lovers were thrilled by the crowning achievements of the Tottenham Hotspur Double side. That Bill Nicholson's legendary group of players is still celebrated today, illustrates two things. One is that comparable success for the club is long overdue; the second is that even now, many people who were there to witness that extraordinary season – whether Tottenham fans or neutrals – make a good case for the Double side being the greatest Britain has ever produced.

Other clubs have matched and even surpassed the single-season trophy haul of the 1960/61 team, but few have played with such captivating flair and skill, and entertained to such a scintillating degree. Across the country vast crowds flocked to see the team dubbed "Super Spurs" raise the game to unprecedented heights of technical team excellence and individual expression.

At the time, the consensus was that winning the league title and FA Cup in the same season was a holy grail that would never be realized. Sure, Aston Villa had done it in 1897. But in a more ruthless and competitive age of dedicated professionalism, securing the championship over a gruelling 42-game campaign and surviving the unpredictability of a six-round knockout competition was felt to be an overambitious aim.

Nicholson and his players, Tottenham legends like Blanchflower, Mackay, Smith, Jones and White, proved it *could* be done. And done in style.

Les Allen scores, Terry Dyson congratulates, and a 61,356 White Hart Lane crowd go wild as Spurs thrash Aston Villa 6-2, 24th September 1960. This was the 10th consecutive victory in the record-setting run that saw Spurs win their first 11 league matches, a sequence that launched Tottenham's bid for the title in unforgettable fashion.

49

The victory over Aston Villa set a new English league record, breaking Hull City's nine-game winning streak set in Division Three (North) in 1948/49. Though not given to premature celebrations before winning a trophy, the players were allowed a glass of champagne to mark the feat. Left to right: Bobby Smith, Terry Dyson, Dave Mackay, Les Allen and John White.

For all the goals, dazzling football and record-breaking runs, winning the title demanded its fair share of victories that owed as much to gritty determination as pure skill. On 25th February 1961, Spurs beat Manchester City thanks to a solitary goal from Terry Medwin. The victory avenged the 1-1 draw back in October that had ended Tottenham's winning streak. Here, Les Allen goes close at Maine Road.

The League Campaign

Nicholson and his coaching team left nothing to chance and preparation was still key. Being instructed to jump to it in training at Cheshunt are Terry Dyson and Les Allen in February 1961. The effort was necessary: a nine-game sequence between January and late March saw Spurs win just three times.

SPURS CHAMPS!

Jones injured—out of Spain game

By BILL HOLDEN

Spurs 2, Sheffield Wednesday 1

THE League Championship trophy will be presented to Spurs on Saturday, April 29.

They won the title without doubt by beating their only challengers, Sheffield Wednesday, in a game where tempers became raw and football was often forgotten.

TOP OF THE TABLE

	P	W	D	L	F.	A.	Pts.
Tottenham	39	30	4	5	111	49	64
Sheffield W.	39	22	12	5	74	41	56
Wolves	40	24	7	9	96	70	55

ON THE WAY . . . Leader Bobby Smith (right) scores Spurs' first goal las' night

MADE IT . . . Les Allen (No. 10) lofts in the second goal to clinch the League crown.

LAZARUS MOBBED AS RANGERS DRAW

£10,000 pay for Haynes riles 'em

By BEN WRIGHT

SEVERAL League clubs are angry at Fulham chairman Tommy Trinder's reported intention to make England skipper Johnny Haynes the highest paid footballer in Europe.

ARSENAL MEN IN IRISH TOUR PARTY

SACKED CAREY TO SUE EVERTON . .

JOHNNY CAREY, former £3,000-a-year manager of Everton, who was sacked four days ago, announced last night that he is to sue the club for alleged breach of contract.

Stitches

Collapsed

Re-bound

★ SPORTS SUMMARY ★

RESULTS

FIXTURES

Left: Any doubts about the title's destination were removed by five successive wins, culminating in victory over Sheffield Wednesday – the same team Spurs had beaten to lift their first title 10 years earlier.

Below: Smiles all round for the champions.

They are the finest club side I've ever seen in the Football League.

Stan Cullis, Wolves manager

—LEGENDS—

Bill Nicholson

No single individual has had as much influence on Tottenham Hotspur as Bill Nicholson. Whether as a championship-winning player, an era-defining manager, or elder statesman of the game, his reputation as one of football's most respected and admired figures stemmed from a near 70-year career of outstanding achievement.

He arrived in north London in 1936, brought down for a trial by chief scout Ben Ives who had heard great things from the club's northern-based talent spotters about a young left-back playing for Scarborough Young Liberals. Nicholson's playing career was interrupted by the war, during which he worked as a PT instructor in the Durham Light Infantry. Switching to the right side of defence when league football resumed, he became an integral member of the Push-and-Run side and earned a solitary England cap as scant recognition of his prowess. Three years as coach continued his managerial apprenticeship before he stepped up to the top job in 1958.

The Double, two further FA Cups, two European trophies and two League Cups made Nicholson far and away Tottenham's greatest ever boss, but even in retirement from management, he continued to serve the club he loved with distinction. Save for a brief spell as a consultant at West Ham, right up to his death in 2004, he was part of the Spurs fabric, whether on match days at White Hart Lane or offering his invaluable advice to youth team players.

Through it all, his philosophy was sacrosanct: football had to be played the right way – the Spurs way.

Bill Nick at a reunion, with his old comrades Ted Ditchburn (centre) and Danny Blanchflower.

GRAND STAND: Spurs' Bill Nicholson stand

THOUSANDS TURN OUT IN TRIBUTE TO LEGEND BILL

By LEE REYNOLDS

SPURS fans turned out in force to pay tribute to Bill Nicholson at a memorial service for the club's greatest manager at White Hart Lane yesterday.

Around 8,000 supporters turned up to pay their respects to Nicholson, who died two weeks ago at the age of 85. Three generations of players and chairman Daniel Levy spoke movingly about Nicholson and how he transformed Spurs into one of Europe's top clubs.

Levy promised supporters that the club would use Nicholson's legacy as their inspiration for the future. "Bill's spirit is with us every step of the way," he said.

OLD PALS: Cliff Jones with Jimmy Greaves

FAVOURITES: Gary Mabbutt with Glenn Hoddle

SAD NOTE: Alan Mullery and Martin Peters

PAYING RESPECT: Ex-skipper Steve Perryman

> *To me, he is all what Tottenham is about.*
> Martin Chivers

> *Bill produced such a dazzling team at White Hart Lane that they won the Double and played the game in a way that was an object lesson to everybody.*
>
> Brian Clough

FOOTBALL –STATS–

Bill Nicholson

Name: William Edward Nicholson OBE

Born: 1919

Died: 2004

Playing Career: 1938-1955

Clubs: Tottenham Hotspur

Tottenham Appearances: 345

Goals: 6

> *It's been my life, Tottenham Hotspur, and I love the club.*
>
> Bill Nicholson

Above: The proud manager with his second great Spurs team in 1968.

Left: In his twilight years, Bill Nick was still a regular presence at the ground. Even in death he is still inextricably attached to the club. The official stadium policy is to ban the scattering of ashes on the pitch, as too many instances would harm the playing surface, but an exception was made for "Mr Tottenham". His remains were cast just beyond the East Stand halfway touchline.

The FA Cup Final 1961

The Double was secured with a 2-0 win over Leicester in the Cup final, thanks to goals from Bobby Smith and Terry Dyson. Ever the perfectionist, Bill Nicholson regretted that the game wasn't won in typical Tottenham style. His team, however, had made the impossible possible.

" *Cup final day is the fans' day.*
Danny Blanchflower "

Left: Danny Blanchflower proudly presents the League Championship trophy and FA Cup from the balcony of Tottenham Town Hall.

Below: Spurs had to wait until the 67th minute before Smith gave them the lead, and this despite Leicester being effectively a man short after an early injury to their right-back Len Chalmers. This was four years before substitutes were allowed in top-flight football, though only then to replace an injured player. Tactical substitutions were not sanctioned until 1967.

–LEGENDS–

Dave Mackay

So much is the legend of Dave Mackay built on his awesome tenacity, bravery, granite-jawed determination, and sheer will to win that it is easy to forget what a gifted footballer he was. The all-action powerhouse in the Double side's midfield engine room, Mackay was arguably the greatest player to don a Tottenham shirt: perhaps only Blanchflower rivals him for all-round talent and importance to the club.

Yet Mackay's reputation as one of the game's great hardmen is undeserved. Never sent off in his career, he could be devastating in the tackle but was never spiteful or dirty. The famous picture of him grabbing a quivering Billy Bremner in 1966 is used to illustrate the supposed way he would take no nonsense from opponents, but it tells only a distorted part of the story. Bremner had just kicked Mackay on the left leg that had been broken twice in nine months two years previously, and understandably the Scotsman felt obliged to remonstrate. The telling point is that it was Mackay's courageousness to come back from such crippling injuries, at a time when medical expertise was nothing like as advanced as it is today, that adds to the true, heroic qualities of the man behind the myth.

"*They say every picture tells a story and so does this image, but it is not the real one.*"

Dave Mackay

A barrel of fierce energy, Mackay was a force of nature both on and off the pitch at Tottenham. He couldn't sit still for the press photographers during a Spurs open training day in July 1965, and no one was more enthusiastic in their celebrations when Spurs won the FA Cup for a fifth time in 1967. Returning to Tottenham in September 1969 with Derby County, he had already reminded his adoring Tottenham crowd what they were missing in the corresponding fixture at Derby earlier in the season: the Rams had thumped Spurs 5-0.

> " He would storm into things with his bloody chest out and that Scottish brawn. "
>
> Bill Nicholson

FOOTBALL -STATS-

Dave Mackay

Name: David Craig Mackay

Born: 1934

Playing Career: 1951-1972

Clubs: Heart of Midlothian, Tottenham Hotspur, Derby County, Swindon Town

Tottenham Appearances: 318

Goals: 51

Tottenham's Swinging Sixties
1961-1969

The timing for Tottenham's Double success appeared perfect. As the country at last bid farewell to the post-war years of austerity and people began to let their hair down, the maximum wage was ended (1961), *Match of the Day* hit the TV screens (1964) and football started to become the showbiz glamour game we know today. Spurs were the best team in Britain and further dazzling success appeared to be there for the taking. The regret is that more league titles were not added to the honours list, as injuries, age and tragedy took their toll on a number of the Double side's greats. But with a further three trophies and pioneering success in Europe, the 1960s was the club's greatest decade.

1961 Jimmy Greaves signs in December for £99,999 1962 Tottenham win FA Cup for second successive season 1962 Spurs just fail to reach the European Cup final 1963 Victory in the European Cup Winners' Cup makes Tottenham the first British side to lift a European trophy 1963 Dave Mackay breaks his leg for the first time 1964 John White is killed, struck by lightning while out on a golf course 1964 Danny Blanchflower retires; Mackay breaks his leg for the second time 1964 Alan Mullery signs from Fulham for £72,500 1965 Roy Low becomes Tottenham's first ever substitute, coming on for Derek Possee against Arsenal in September 1965 Jimmy Greaves finishes as top scorer in Division One for third successive season 1966 Mike England signs for £95,000 1967 Spurs win the FA Cup for fifth time 1968 Bill Nicholson completes a decade as Spurs manager 1968 Seats installed in the top tier of the Paxton Road end and stand linked up with the West Stand 1969 Steve Perryman makes his debut for Spurs, aged 17

Big news in the media: Tottenham were the subject of a celebratory book called *Spurs 1961*. Avidly reading are left to right: Terry Dyson, Les Allen, Bill Brown, Danny Blanchflower and Bobby Smith.

Showing how comfortable he was with a tennis ball as much as a football, Maurice Norman plays "keep-uppy" by the team

Right: Nicholson made only one significant addition to the line-up, signing Jimmy Greaves in December 1961 (third right). The England striker joins in the relaxed fun as Bobby Smith (fourth from left) gets familiar with Peter Baker.

Below: The 1961/62 season got under way with a special Charity Shield fixture against a select FA XI, held as part of Tottenham's league and cup double celebrations. Spurs won 3-2.

–LEGENDS–

Bobby Smith, Cliff Jones and John White

Right: Tottenham's second highest goalscorer is often described as a "traditional English centre-forward" but in common with Dave Mackay that detracts from the depth of his overall talent. Big and powerful Smith certainly was, but it was his technique that earned him as many goals as his strength; 33 goals during the Double season and 13 goals in 15 internationals with England confirm how prolific he was on any stage. Smith was also brave, taking pain-killing injections in the Tottenham cause (some unbeknown to Nicholson).

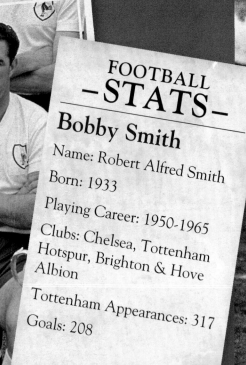

FOOTBALL –STATS–
Bobby Smith

Name: Robert Alfred Smith

Born: 1933

Playing Career: 1950-1965

Clubs: Chelsea, Tottenham Hotspur, Brighton & Hove Albion

Tottenham Appearances: 317

Goals: 208

Cliff Jones' 10-year Tottenham career ranks as one of the club's most successful. Signed for £35,000 in 1958, he left with five major honours and was one of the first unused substitutes to win a medal (having remained on the bench for the 1967 FA Cup). Throughout his time at Spurs he was one of the favourites among team-mates and crowd. Fearless, fast, and brilliant on the ball, the Welshman was considered by many to be the best left-winger in the world.

Of all the losses that the Double side experienced, none was more keenly felt, nor put football into such trivial context, as the tragic death of John White. White, dubbed "the Ghost of White Hart Lane" for his almost spectral ability to arrive just at the right time into attacking positions, was an inside-right of sublime skill and vision, an ever-present in 1960/61, and was on the threshold of even greater performances when he was killed on 21st July 1964, struck by lightning while out playing golf at Crews Hill, Middlesex. His young family had lost a loving husband and father; his team-mates were grief-stricken; Bill Nicholson crushed. Spurs and football had lost one of the game's brightest stars.

John White wasn't just of Spurs and Scotland—he belonged to the whole world of Soccer, one of the great players of our time.

Dropped points in the spring meant Spurs missed out on a second successive title, but compensation came with a second successive FA Cup triumph, as Spurs beat Burnley 3-1. Danny Blanchflower beats Adam Blacklaw from the spot to wrap up the victory.

Left: In front of the massed ranks of Spurs supporters, John White and Maurice Norman (right) take the acclaim.

Right: Bill Nick sportingly offers Jimmy Anderson, captain of his defeated opponents, a sup of champagne from the cup.

Peter Baker (holding the cup) and Bill Nicholson, cheered by some of the vast crowd that greeted the Spurs side during their victory parade along Tottenham High Road.

The People's Game

Bumper crowds were a feature of the decade as Tottenham fans revelled in the club's glory days. These youngsters brandishing their tickets for the FA Cup quarter-final against Aston Villa were wise to have started queuing at 5.30am – 64,000 were packed into White Hart Lane to see the 2-0 win on 10th March 1962.

For all the technological advances of the era that Labour leader and later prime minister Harold Wilson heralded as "the white heat of technology', more traditional apparatus such as rattles was still a feature of the White Hart Lane terraces in 1964.

Fans shared in the success, as with this group waiting to see their heroes during the 1962 victory parade.

Bill Nicholson always said to us that the most important people in the stadium were not the players, not the management, but the supporters. These people worked 40 hours a week and would then come out and support us and, even more so in those days, their money would pay our wages. The club is a huge part of the community and we were made aware of our responsibilities to them.

Cliff Jones

—LEGENDS—

Jimmy Greaves

England's greatest ever goalscorer? There are plenty of claimants to the crown but few would begrudge Jimmy Greaves the title of number one. This avuncular cockney was a goalscoring machine and averaged an astonishing 70% goals-to-games ratio during his magnificent Spurs career. Greaves was to the manor born at Tottenham, an artist whose ruthless efficiency in the penalty area was matched only by his brilliant technique.

Rescued from a miserable spell in Italian football by Bill Nick in December 1961, Greaves was bought for £99,999 in order not to burden him with the tag of becoming the game's first £100,000 player. It probably wouldn't have mattered. Coolness personified, he scored a hat-trick on his Spurs debut, scored in the 1962 FA Cup final, and scored in his first FA Cup game for Spurs. In his nine seasons at the Lane he finished as the Division One top scorer four times – no one in Tottenham's long history before or since has come close to matching his achievements.

> " *He would pass the ball into the net.*
> Bill Nicholson "

> " *He was always very calm, very collected, and where scoring goals was concerned, he was a Picasso.*
> Clive Allen "

Below: Whatever the stage, Greaves prospered with Spurs, scoring here at Wembley in the 1962 FA Cup final after just three minutes.

Celebrating the 1967 FA Cup semi-final win over Nottingham Forest with a beer close at hand. Greaves's well-documented problems with alcohol helped to bring his playing career to a premature end, but he recovered to carve out a successful second career as a TV pundit and speaker.

Left: December 1961 and manager Bill Nicholson brings Greaves to Spurs.

Bottom Left: Greaves's prolific scoring rate meant that within just two seasons at Spurs he was closing in on 200 career league goals – at the age of just 23.

FOOTBALL –STATS–

Jimmy Greaves

Name: James Peter Greaves

Born: 1940

Playing Career: 1955-1971

Clubs: Chelsea, AC Milan, Tottenham Hotspur, West Ham United

Tottenham Appearances: 380

Goals: 266

It's a Funny Old Game

In recent years Jimmy Greaves has proved to be an entertaining host, a natural presenter and a fine stand-up comedian ~~on~~ the football speaking circuit. Back in the 1960s he was similarly comfortable at exclusive social occasions, and adept at disp~~laying a~~ sense of comic timing almost as good as his predatory goalscoring instinct in the box.

Invited to the House of Commons by Tottenham MP Alan Brown for a pre-Cup final reception in 1962, Greavsie cou~~ld not~~ resist an impromptu kick about in one of the Commons' tea rooms (above) with Liverpool MP Bessie Braddock. Distinc~~tly~~ unimpressed is an attendant waitress, but she might have cheered up to learn that the ball was later autographed by the

Top Left: Paying a house call to No 10 Downing Street and Prime Minister Harold Wilson in February 1965 are Cliff Jones and Jimmy Greaves. The pair joined a number of other sports celebrities, including boxer Billy Walker, to mark the launch of the Sports Council.

Top Right: Raising a glass with Dave Mackay (left) and Danny Blanchflower (centre) at the club's Christmas Party in 1961.

Left: In 1969, as his career at Spurs drew to an end, Greaves was given time off by Bill Nicholson to take part in the *Mirror's* World Cup rally. The country's most famous striker provided back-up to Tony Fall driving a Ford Escort for the car giant's works team – it's difficult to imagine Sir Alex Ferguson allowing Wayne Rooney quite the same freedom.

The gruelling and dangerous 16,000-mile rally left Wembley stadium on 19th April and finished in Mexico City just in time for the start of the 1970 World Cup. Looking somewhat uncertain behind the wheel, Greaves gets in some much-needed practice on the BSM "Skid Pan" at Brands Hatch.

A Footballer's Life...

Football in the 1960s offered all sorts of opportunities to players but also made exacting demands. The famous Double side line up for their flu inoculation on 25th October 1962.

Peter Baker gets the needle while Dave Mackay waits his turn.

Freed from the restrictions of the maximum wage, many footballers looked to invest their earnings in outside interests – even if it meant working indirectly for other clubs. Bill Brown followed in the footsteps of his predecessor in the Spurs goal, Ted Ditchburn, and went into business, setting up a printing company. Here, he shows West Ham players Ron Boyce (left), Ken Brown and John Lyle (right) proofs of the new West Ham official handbook produced at Brown's factory.

Left: Flat caps, roll-ups and trips home on the No 279 bus with the fans had become a thing of the past. Relaxing in private-coach luxury and enjoying his pipe is a dapper Greaves in May 1965, returning from England training at Roehampton.

Fame is the Spur   Jimmy Greaves signs autographs outside White Hart Lane in March 1964

WAGS,
1960s Style

Right: As footballers increasingly became part of the showbiz world, so their love lives also came under the media's gaze. In January 1967, Spurs goalkeeper Pat Jennings tied the knot with Eleanor Toner, at St Mary's Church, Hampstead. Eleanor herself was something of a celebrity as a recording artist and singer with the Hilton Showband. Pat and Eleanor – the Posh and Becks of their day.

Above: Danny Blanchflower was a favourite celebrity subject and his marriage to wife number three, nurse Avrielle Hunter, in December 1963, was featured in the news and not the sports pages. Blanchflower, however, kept his counsel. "I'm a shy and reticent sort of a fellow about certain things," he said.

When future Spurs boss and then Arsenal player George Graham (centre) wed Marie Zia on 16th September 1967, another future Spurs boss was on hand to perform best-man duties – Terry Venables. Both players then featured in the north London derby a few hours later. Chelsea's John Hollins, for some strange reason, holds a fluffy owl.

Left: As befitted a football club that was no stranger to glamour, Tottenham Hotspur drew supporters from all sorts of backgrounds and fields. Here, rubbing dress-suited shoulders with Mike England (left) and Pat Jennings (right) is gangland figure Freddie Foreman, together at the Royal Garden Hotel, Kensington.

Below Left: Tottenham's association with records didn't start with Chas and Dave. In 1961 The Totnamites released 'Tip Top Tottenham Hotspur' and six years later the players themselves decided to go into the studio to make an album of sing-along old standards. Leading a clearly well-refreshed choir is Jimmy Greaves, as the team record for posterity such favourites as 'Maybe It's Because I'm a Londoner', 'Strolling', 'I Belong to Glasgow' and 'Glory Glory Hallelujah'.

FOOTBALL
–STATS–

Pat Jennings

Name: Patrick Anthony Jennings MBE

Born: 1945

Playing Career: 1963-1985

Clubs: Watford, Tottenham Hotspur, Arsenal

Tottenham Appearances: 591

Goals: 1

So many other people depend on me doing well.

Pat Jennings

78

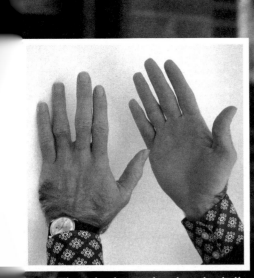

Inset: The safest biggest hands in football, in close-up.

—LEGENDS—

Above: Signing autographs for young fans in Belfast. Few players were as popular throughout the game as Jennings.

Pat Jennings

Spurs have a proud tradition of fielding great goalkeepers, and arguably Pat Jennings was the greatest of them all. Second only to Steve Perryman in the number of all-time Tottenham appearances, Jennings was the best goalkeeper in the world at his peak, and displayed a level of outstanding consistency throughout his long and distinguished career that included 119 caps for Northern Ireland during 22 years of international duty.

Signed from Watford in 1964 for £27,000 as the successor to Bill Brown, Jennings struggled at first but soon became the all-round ideal keeper. With an impressive physique honed with a Newry timber gang, he was an athletic and commanding presence, displaying a resolute determination that brought assurance to team-mates. He was also a phenomenal shot-stopper, blessed with huge hands for which the ball had an almost magnetic attraction. He could also kick the ball like no other, famously scoring against Manchester United in the 1967 Charity Shield with one monster drop kick.

Jennings actually spent two spells at White Hart Lane. In difficult circumstances (manager Keith Burkinshaw admitted letting him go was a mistake), Jennings made the short trip across north London to Highbury in 1977, where he ably tended the Arsenal goal for six years. Returning to his natural home in 1983 and going on to become a coach at Spurs, Jennings is one of the few players to have crossed the north London divide and remained popular at both clubs.

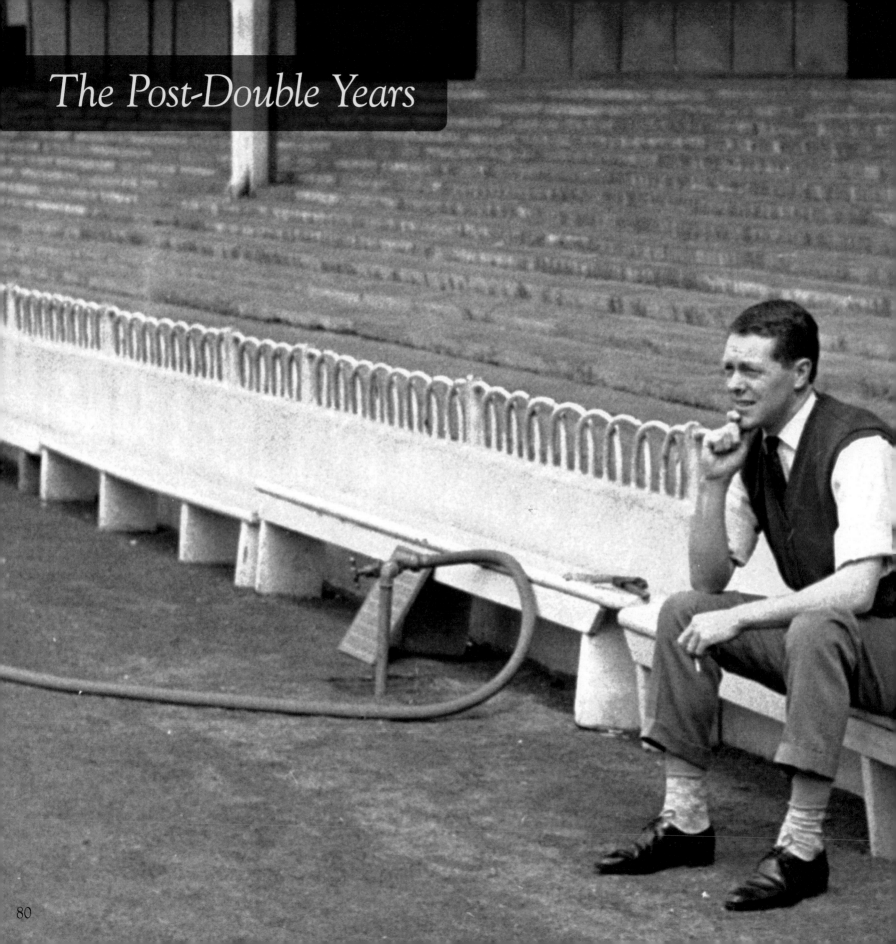

anything else was going to be something of an anti climax. Tottenham just missed out on a second successive Double in the next campaign, but the rest of the decade was full of many highs – though, sadly, also some lows.

Les Allen caught in thoughtful mood, sitting alone at White Hart Lane in May 1962.

The Cruel Game

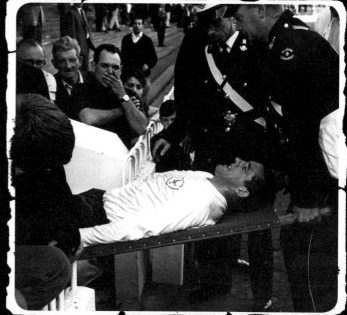

Above: Carried from the pitch in agony, a distraught fan looking on, Mackay's first thought was for his manager. "Don't let Bill Nick know," he said, worried that his predicament would distract Nicholson from the first-team game at West Ham, "not yet."

Above: Calamity struck when, having just returned to action nine months after the first injury, Mackay's left leg was again broken in a reserve match against Shrewsbury. A concerned referee Peter Songhurst calls for aid.

Right: Resting at home after his first break, Mackay, with his children Valerie (4) and Derek (6), is visited by Spurs team-mates Terry Dyson (left) and Bobby Smith at his Enfield home.

Spurs lost a number of players after the Double, but no absence proved to be as costly as Dave Mackay's, whose twice-broken leg effectively ruled him out for two years. Had Mackay been fit and present, Spurs might well have landed the league title again.

The first break came after a controversial tackle from Noel Cantwell in the second leg of a first-round Cup Winners' Cup meeting with Manchester United in December 1963, ruling Mackay out for the rest of the season. Bill Nicholson said, "We shall not panic. We shall not buy for the sake of buying. Mackay's injury is a tremendous blow to us but it's not the end of the world."

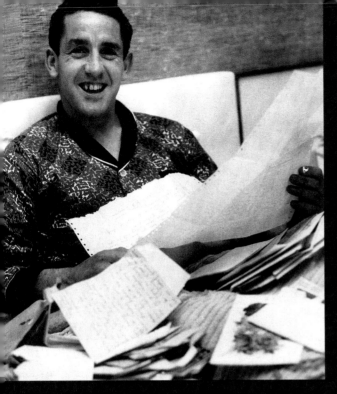

Back in hospital Mackay caught up with some of the thousands of letters he had received from fans.

November 1964 and Mackay leaves hospital with his daughter Valerie, ready to begin his second comeback.

The long hard slog back to fitness paid dividends. Within two years, Mackay was a winner with Spurs once more.

> *They say tough men don't cry, but believe me they do.*
>
> Alan Mullery describing
> Bill Nicholson's reaction to
> news of Mackay's second leg break

The mid-1960s matches between Tottenham and Manchester United were the biggest clashes of their day: north versus south; Nicholson's Glory-Glory Lilywhites versus the Busby Babes; the Double winners versus the soon-to-be European Cup winners. In the season of 1965/66 the teams produced a pair of epic encounters, with both sides winning 5-1 at home. Here, Jimmy Greaves goes for goal at White Hart Lane on 16th October 1965.

Terry Venables was a youthful new recruit to Spurs in May 1966. Signed from Chelsea for £80,000, he struggled to fill some pretty substantial midfield gaps vacated by various members of the Double side. They were hard acts to follow, and Venables made more of an impact at Spurs as manager over 20 years later.

Above: Jimmy Greaves celebrates after scoring from the spot in the April 1966 league clash with Northampton. In doing so, Greaves maintained his record of scoring against every Division One club he had faced.

Right: Back in the 1960s, goal celebrations could often prompt spectators to spill unhindered onto the pitch – even those armed with a walking stick. Keith Weller (no 11) joins in the fun with Alan Gilzean and Terry Venables as Spurs beat that season's champions Manchester United 2-1 in September 1966.

–LEGENDS–

Alan Mullery

Like Terry Venables, when he arrived at Spurs Alan Mullery was burdened by the weight of expectation in stepping into the illustrious shoes of the likes of Danny Blanchflower. Initially, Mullery laboured to win the fans over but his perseverance was rewarded when his combative, all-action style earned him the nickname "Tank", and he became a firm terrace favourite.

When Mackay departed, Mullery was the obvious and deserved choice to become captain, a role he fulfilled with distinction, leading Spurs to further success in the League Cup (1971) and UEFA Cup (1972), in the latter of which he scored with a typically brave header.

> "Everything at Tottenham was on a large scale. Fulham was fun. Tottenham was business. At Spurs you were expected to win things.
>
> Alan Mullery

FOOTBALL –STATS–

Alan Mullery

Name: Alan Patrick Mullery MBE

Born: 1941

Playing Career: 1958-1976

Clubs: Fulham, Tottenham Hotspur

Tottenham Appearances: 374

Goals: 30

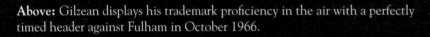

Above: Gilzean displays his trademark proficiency in the air with a perfectly timed header against Fulham in October 1966.

–LEGENDS–

Alan Gilzean

The original "King of White Hart Lane", Alan Gilzean boasted an elegant yet deceptively powerful attacking style all of his own. Subtle he may have been, but Gilzean still gave Scottish, English and European defences nightmares for the best part of 13 years. A brilliant partner to Jimmy Greaves, the pair became known as the G-Men for their devastating displays of the striker's art, with Gilzean the skilled swordsman setting Greaves up for his rapier finishes. Equally effective in tandem with Martin Chivers, "Gilly" was perhaps at his best in the air, with _____ingly accurate headers delivered off that

FOOTBALL –STATS–

Alan Gilzean

Name: Alan John Gilzean

Born: 1938

Playing Career: 1957-1974

Clubs: Dundee, Tottenham Hotspur

Tottenham Appearances: 429

Goals: 133

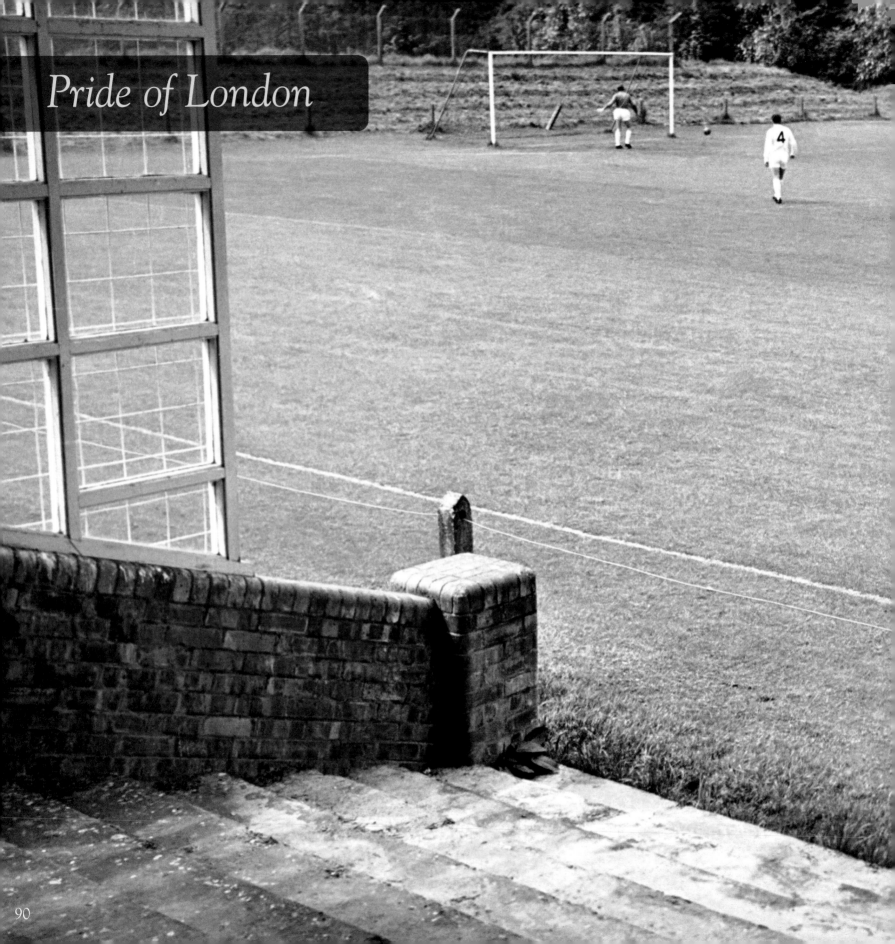

The calm before the storm . . . On the eve of the 1967 FA
Cup final against Chelsea, Spurs players get in some last-
minute training at a deserted Cheshunt.

91

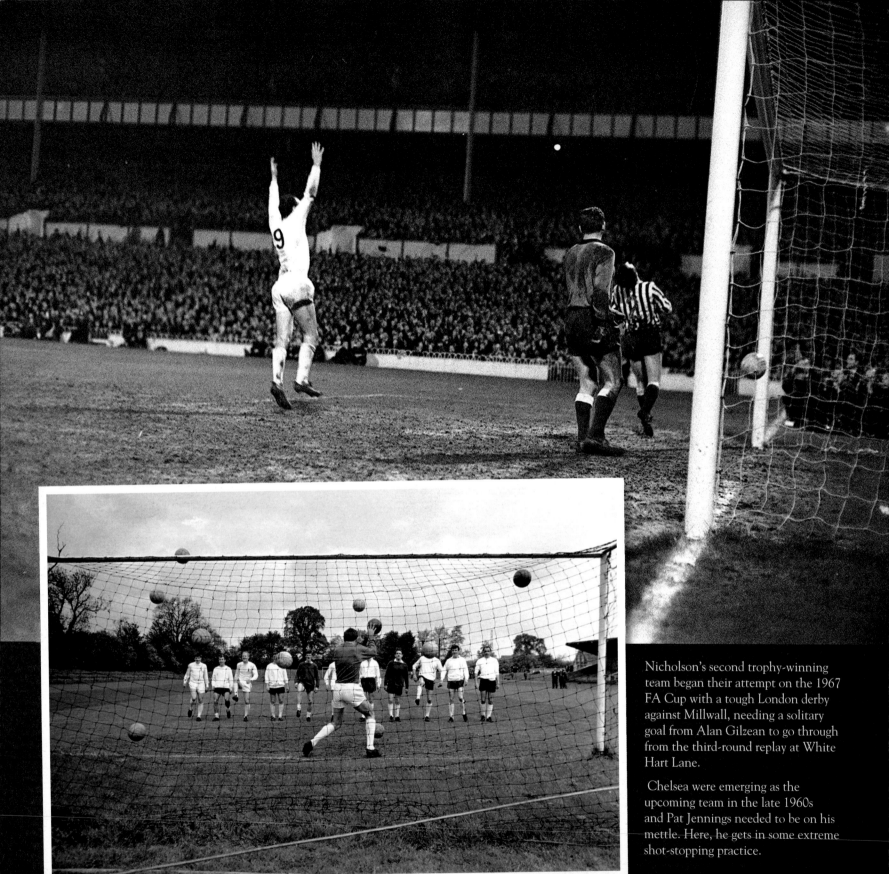

Nicholson's second trophy-winning team began their attempt on the 1967 FA Cup with a tough London derby against Millwall, needing a solitary goal from Alan Gilzean to go through from the third-round replay at White Hart Lane.

Chelsea were emerging as the upcoming team in the late 1960s and Pat Jennings needed to be on his mettle. Here, he gets in some extreme shot-stopping practice.

CHELSEA (Blue shirts, blue shorts)

1. PETER BONETTI

2. ALLAN HARRIS

3. EDDIE McCREADIE

4. JOHN HOLLINS

5. MARVIN HINTON

6. RON HARRIS (Captain)

7. CHARLIE COOKE

8. BOBBY TAMBLING

9. TOMMY BALDWIN

10. TONY HATELEY

11. JOHN BOYLE

TOTTENHAM HOTSPUR (White shirts, white shorts)

1. PAT JENNINGS

2. JOE KINNEAR

3. CYRIL KNOWLES

4. ALAN MULLERY

5. MIKE ENGLAND

6. DAVE MACKAY (Captain)

7. JIMMY ROBERTSON

8. JIMMY GREAVES

9. ALAN GILZEAN

10. TERRY VENABLES

11. FRANK SAUL

Left: Pen portraits by the *Daily Mirror's* Sallon briefed readers on the personnel competing in the first FA Cup final between two London sides.

Below: Goalscorer Jimmy Robertson is foiled this time by Eddie McCreadie.

Venables, Greaves and Mullery celebrate in the dressing room after the 2-1 victory. Goals from Jimmy Robertson and Frank Saul sealed what was, in truth, an emphatic win, secured with an impressive all-round team display.

Back on the well-worn White Hart Lane victory parade, Spurs showed off yet another trophy to their adoring fans. Facing the camera are Mike England (left), and Terry Venables, clasping an ecstatic Dave Mackay.

Putting their left (and right) feet in and doing the hokey-cokey are assorted Spurs players and wives, letting their hair down at the post-match reception at the Hilton Hotel.

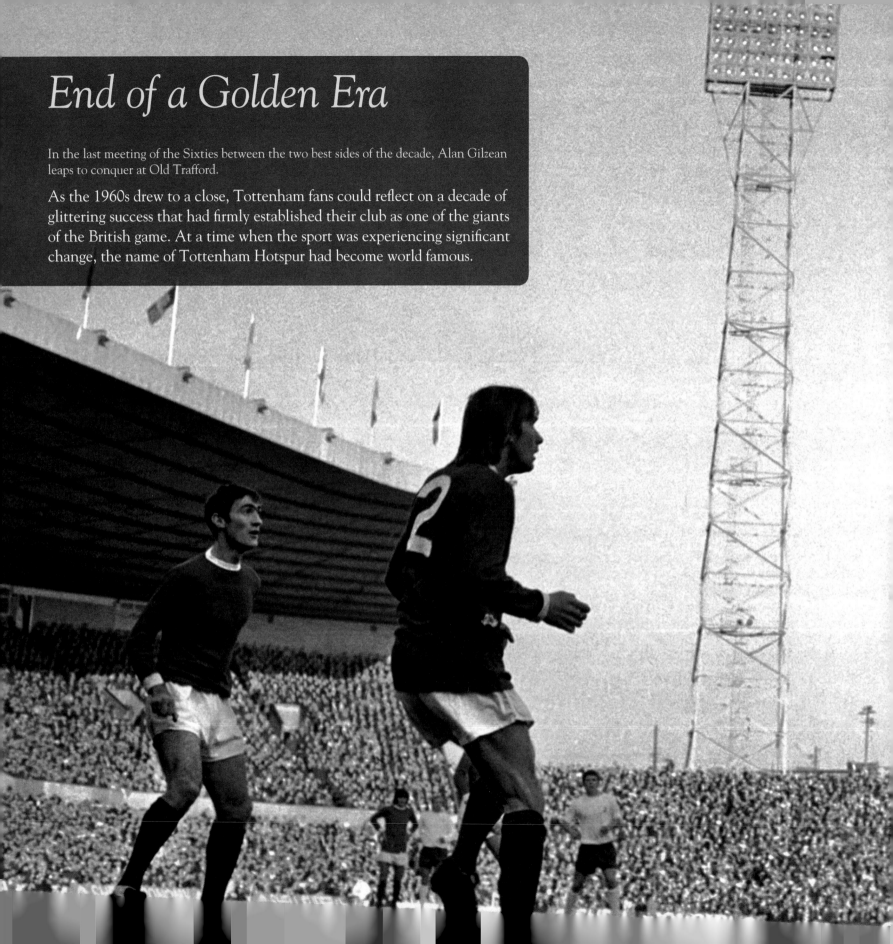

End of a Golden Era

In the last meeting of the Sixties between the two best sides of the decade, Alan Gilzean leaps to conquer at Old Trafford.

As the 1960s drew to a close, Tottenham fans could reflect on a decade of glittering success that had firmly established their club as one of the giants of the British game. At a time when the sport was experiencing significant change, the name of Tottenham Hotspur had become world famous.

Above: Spurs and Manchester City players pick up pieces of broken glass from the White Hart Lane pitch in December 1968, after bottles were thrown from the terraces. Hooliganism was becoming an increasingly common occurrence at English football grounds.

Right: Alan Gilzean troops off after receiving his marching orders in the league tussle with Leeds at Elland Road in April 1968. Dismissals were still a relatively rare occurrence – Frank Saul's sending-off in 1965 was the first for Spurs in the league since that of Cecil Poynton in 1928.

Left: An aerial battle from the FA Cup fourth-round win over Preston in February 1968.

Below: Pat Jennings leaps to his right to deny Bobby Charlton from the penalty spot at White Hart Lane but he couldn't prevent a 2-1 defeat for Spurs, in February 1968.

Nights of Glory

Danny Blanchflower scores from the spot in the epic European Cup encounter against the mighty Benfica, 5th April 1962.

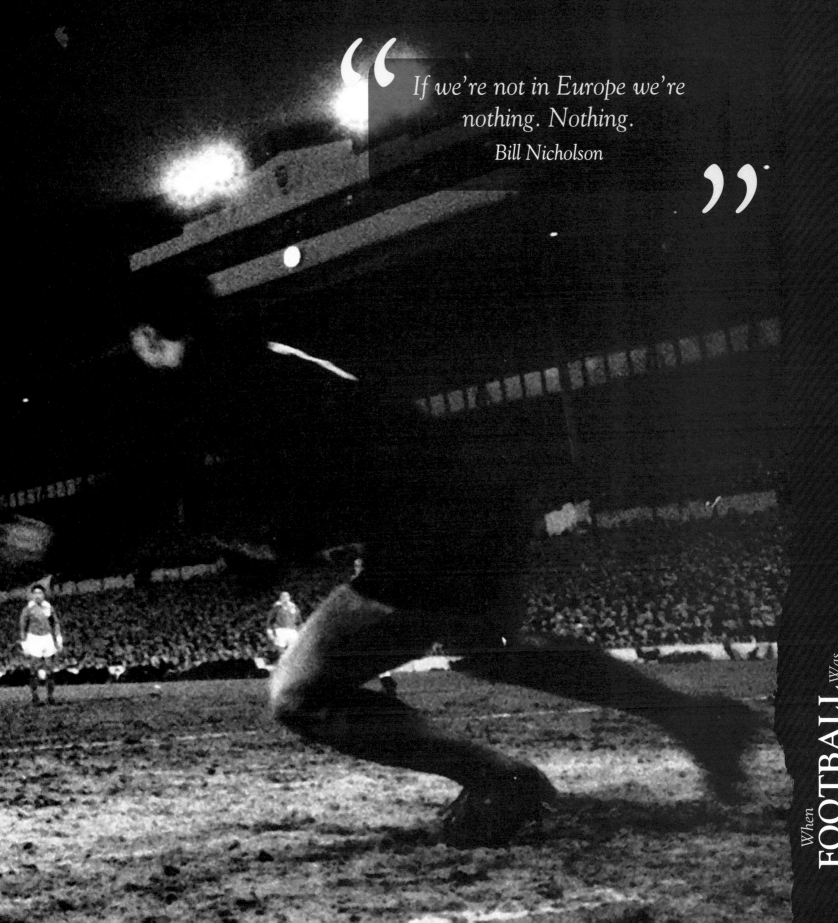

" *If we're not in Europe we're nothing. Nothing.*
Bill Nicholson "

As a venue, White Hart Lane has always had a sense of theatre. Drama, star names and glamour and – as even the most devoted fan would concede – a fair share of melodrama and farce seem to be as much a part of the stadium's fabric as concrete and steel. But the fluctuating fortunes of Tottenham have never appeared more dramatic than under the intense glare of floodlights amid the famous "glory glory" nights of European games.

Such evenings have always had something special about them, the north London air crackling with a degree of anticipation and excitement rarely matched by the day-to-day domestic games. As winners of the 1963 Cup Winners' Cup, Spurs have the pioneering distinction of being the first British side to land a European trophy. Sadly, the financial realities of the modern game have meant it is the Premier League that now counts above all else and until Tottenham qualify for the Champions League, competing in Europe has lost some of its sheen. But the memory of the classic games of the past will never fade.

Tottenham had warmed up for their continental adventures in preceding years with a number of tours to mainland Europe, including Austria, West Germany and the USSR. In November 1960 Spurs entertained one of the Soviet Union's most famous sides, Dinamo Tibilisi, in a friendly under the White Hart Lane floodlights. The hosts gave some indication of what the rest of Europe could expect with a crushing 5-2 win, with two of the goals

The First Campaign

Tottenham's entry into the European Cup sparked great anticipation, not just in north London but throughout English football. The insularity of the domestic governing bodies had, in previous years, held other clubs back – Chelsea had been prevented by the Football League from taking part in 1955, supposedly on the grounds of fixture congestion. But by 1961, after Manchester United and Wolves had tried to land the big prize, such "official" suspicions had eased. Spurs were seen as the side most likely to show what English football was made of. All Europe was about to find out.

Left: Arguably the most memorable game of the 1961/62 European campaign was the preliminary round, second-leg tie on 20th September against Górnik Zabrze of Poland. Spurs had slumped to a shock 4-2 defeat in the first leg, a result that infuriated Bill Nicholson and led to unjustified accusations from the Poles that Tottenham were "no angels" after a tackle by Mackay injured Górnik's left-half Kowalski.

In response, Spurs fans Peter Kirby, Dave Casey and Mike Curly dressed up in heavenly attire to parade around the pitch for the return, and offer proof of Tottenham's saintly qualities. It is believed that this display also led to the first sustained singing of the Spurs anthem 'Glory Glory Hallelujah'.

The vocal support worked. Spurs simply destroyed Górnik 8-1, in front of a crowd that many who were there maintain was far in excess of the official 56,737 (the noise was described as "titanic" by the author's father). Spilling onto the pitch after the final whistle are two of the "Tottenham angels", alongside ecstatic fellow supporters.

Right: Spurs eventually reached the semi-final to meet the holders, Benfica. Despite losing 3-1 in the first leg (Tottenham had two goals controversially disallowed), expectation reached fever pitch for the return leg. At White Hart Lane thousands queued for tickets; the stage was set for one of the greatest games in Tottenham Hotspur's history.

105

Right: Action from the Benfica home leg. The visitors' legendary centre-half Germano Luís de Figueiredo (second from right) looks on helplessly in the face of yet another Tottenham attack.

Far Right: A despondent Blanchflower and White leave the field, their European dream over – for now.

Below: In one of many hotly disputed moments in the tie, Jimmy Greaves is ruled offside as he beats goalkeeper Pereira.

'It was the hardest game of my life.'
Benfica manager, Bela Guttman

"

In the final analysis, it was a defeat – but if a loss can ever be described as glorious then this was it. On an unforgettable night, Spurs did everything but score the elusive fourth goal that would have taken Benfica to extra time. A Blanchflower penalty and a Bobby Smith strike ensured a 2-1 win on the night but Spurs went out 4-3 on aggregate, having seen yet another goal disallowed and three attempts come off the woodwork.

"Come on you Spurs!" Up to 2009, Tottenham Hotspur had competed in 16 different European campaigns, providing supporters with some of the most enjoyable footballing nights in the club's history, as these supporters illustrate during the 1962 Cup Winners' Cup meeting with Glasgow Rangers. Even greater delights lay ahead.

Tottenham's Battle of Britain

Right: Contests between top English and Scottish teams have become relatively common fixtures in recent years, but in 1962, the Cup Winners' Cup clash between Spurs and Rangers had all the trappings of a truly special occasion. Demand for tickets was, as always, very high. Plenty of Scots made the trip to the capital for the first leg which Tottenham won 5-2, before the Londoners completed an aggregate 8-4 win in Glasgow. Here, Rangers' manager Scot Symon greets Spurs' manager Bill Nicholson at the visitors' hotel.

Left: Rangers fans make their presence felt at White Hart Lane with a banner and a skirl of bagpipes.

Below: The frantic rush to buy tickets.

EUROPEAN CUP WINNERS CUP

TOTTENHAM HOTSPUR v RANGERS F.C.

WEDNESDAY, 31st OCTOBER, 1962

SALE OF GROUND TICKETS

SUNDAY 28th OCTOBER commencing 1 p.m.

NO QUEUEING BEFORE 10 A.M.

POLICE MAY DISPERSE PERSONS CONGREGATING BEFORE THIS TIME

Cliff Jones climbs high with a headed effort on the Rangers' goal.

Magnanimous in victory, Spurs form a guard of honour.

Danny Blanchflower shakes hands and exchanges pennants with his counterpart Bobby Shearer.

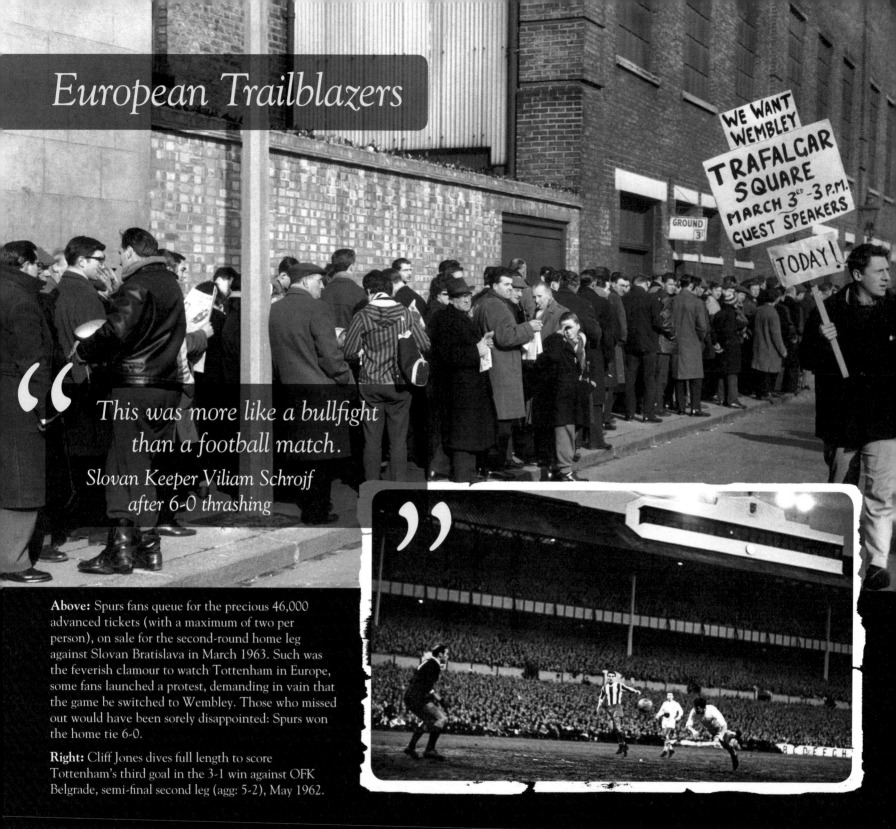

European Trailblazers

> *"This was more like a bullfight than a football match.*
>
> Slovan Keeper Viliam Schrojf
> after 6-0 thrashing *"*

Above: Spurs fans queue for the precious 46,000 advanced tickets (with a maximum of two per person), on sale for the second-round home leg against Slovan Bratislava in March 1963. Such was the feverish clamour to watch Tottenham in Europe, some fans launched a protest, demanding in vain that the game be switched to Wembley. Those who missed out would have been sorely disappointed: Spurs won the home tie 6-0.

Right: Cliff Jones dives full length to score Tottenham's third goal in the 3-1 win against OFK Belgrade, semi-final second leg (agg: 5-2), May 1962.

The 1962/63 European Cup Winners' Cup was to prove a watershed, not just for Tottenham but for English football as a whole. Spurs rampaged through the rounds, scoring 19 goals in six games, before another five-goal salvo saw off Atletico Madrid in the final, earning Tottenham a unique distinction, as the first British club to win a major trophy in European football.

.. AND SUDDENLY TIRED TOTTENHAM ARE THE TOAST OF SOCCER AGAIN!

—MADRID MAULED 5-1

Greaves sparks off the great goal riot..

From KEN JONES   Rotterdam, Wednesday

SUPER Spurs won the European Cup Winners' Cup here tonight with this five-goal massacre of Madrid—and became the first British club to carry off one of Europe's top Soccer trophies.

It was in the tradition of true champions that Spurs came bursting back to write another glorious chapter in their history.

Their League hopes gone, this Cup Final at the Feyenoord Stadium was their last bridgehead into Europe next season.

And suddenly a tired team found the extra energy, courage, and, above all, the extra skill that has taken them to the summit of Soccer.

The scoreline hides the very real fact that for fifteen nail-biting minutes in the second half they suddenly seemed to have "gone."

But it does no injustice to a team smarting under the jibes that they were finished as a football force who came back to hit Soccer's high spots again.

At times Spurs were superb. Their cool, controlled football was from the mould of their great days.

And after weeks of fumbling in attack the forwards suddenly clicked again.

Superb

Remember that Spurs were without powerhouse wing half Dave Mackay, who was injured.

Remember that four years at the top has sapped their stamina—and we may never see this side playing in big game competition again.

But above all remember the superb skill. The gazelle-like runs of Cliff Jones looking every inch the perfect winger as he demoralised the Atletico defence.

The return to form of goal ace Jimmy Greaves and the comeback of schemer John White.

The storming centre half play of mighty Maurice Norman and the cheek and courage of little Terry Dyson, playing his best ever game for Spurs.

Perfect

Their first goal in the 16th minute was one I shall never forget. Centre forward Bobby Smith, unflinching in the face of some rugged tackles by centre half Griffa, sent Jones bulleting to the right corner flag.

The Welshman's cross was inch perfect and Greaves batted the ball home on the run.

In the 32nd minute Dyson hooked one back from the by-line and White, with studied calm, cracked the ball into the roof of the net.

The Spaniards needed a quick goal at the start of the second half, and they got it in the forty-sixth minute.

Left back Ron Henry punched a shot away from under the bar, and left winger Collar hammered home the penalty kick.

Suddenly Spurs were in trouble. Goalkeeper Bill Brown had to make a desperate kick away save.

And then Henry, playing all the second half with strained ligaments in his left knee, headed one off the line from inside left Mendoza.

Spurs needed luck. And they got it in the sixty-ninth minute when Dyson suddenly snatched an amazing goal.

A quick turn took him inside the full back, and when he hung his cross high under the bar goalkeeper Madinabeyta backhanded the ball into his own net.

Twelve minutes from time the fans were singing "Glory, Glory Hallelujah" as Spurs made it safe when Dyson's cross was bludgeoned home on the far post by Greaves.

And fittingly it was Dyson who got the fifth three minutes from time with a shot from the edge of the area.

Spurs manager Bill Nicholson said afterwards: "Dyson played better than I have ever seen him. Norman and Marchi were terrific.

Fluke

"But don't forget it was that third goal—a fluke that clinched it. We started to get the ball again then.

"I am tremendously proud for the players and my club to be the first manager of a British team to win a European title."

Leo Horn, the Dutch referee, who watched the game, said:

"This was the best performance I have ever seen from an English club. Why doesn't your national team play like this?"

TOTTENHAM HOTSPUR .. 5	
Greaves (16 mins, 78), White (32), Dyson (69, 87).	
ATLETICO MADRID .. 1	
Collar (46, pen.).	
H-T: 2—0	

Jimmy Greaves comes galloping in to score his second goal, beating full backs Rivilla and Rodriguez.

HALLELUJAH! EUROPEAN CUP WINNERS' CUP COMES TO WHITE HART LANE

GLORIOUS SPURS

Tennis bogey laid

BATTLING BILLY SLAMS FORBES

From C. M. JONES - - - - Paris, Wednesday

BRITISH Davis Cup player Billy Knight broke a nine-year bogey by beating South Africa's Gordon Forbes 1—6, 7—5, 4—6, 8—4, 6—0 in the second round of the French championships here today.

Last time Billy beat Forbes was way back in 1954 at Bournemouth, yet when Knight came off the centre court he grumbled: "What a terrible match."

And later he told team manager Dan Maskell: "I just don't know how I won."

The answer is old-fashioned British guts.

The 6ft. 3in. Forbes usually beats Knight by hitting every ball to the backhand and attacking him from the net.

Hit Back

And when Gordon took the first set 6—1 it looked like the old, old story. But a swirling wind harmed the South African's aim, and Billy was able to cover his backhand weakness and take the second set.

He lost the third, but showed tremendous spirit to square the match after being 2—4 down in the fourth set.

Fine passing shots gave Billy a break for 2—0 in the final set, and after that he won in a canter.

Bobby Wilson and Mike Sangster also won their matches.

SOCCER

FA YOUTH CUP—Fifth-round Replay: Arsenal 0, Wolverhampton 4 (Roberts 2, Clements, Holder).

Skipper Danny Blanchflower, chaired by his jubilant team-mates, gets a firm grip on the gleaming European Cup Winners' Cup. Will it be bubbling with champagne? "No," said Danny. "It'll be Coca-Cola! That's my usual drink.

Tottenham's very own VE Day. Missing the injured Dave Mackay, and with the 37-year-old Danny Blanchflower requiring an injection to be passed fit, Spurs faced an uphill struggle against the cup-holders. Spirits were hardly lifted by a somewhat sombre pre-match team talk from Bill Nick that concentrated on Atletico's strengths. Blanchflower promptly restored confidence with a rousing dressing room address talking up his own side's chances. It worked. The game became known as Dyson's final, after the diminutive winger, standing just 5ft 3in in his socks, played the game of his life and scored twice in a 5-2 rout.

Above: Ecstatic fans briefly get their hands on the trophy at the gates of White Hart Lane.

Below: Double goalscorers Jimmy Greaves and Terry Dyson are all smiles. John White also got on the scoresheet.

Above: Hail the conquering jet-set heroes . . . Tottenham return triumphant to London with the cup. Front to back are: Tony Marchi holding the cup, Bill Brown, Bobby Smith, Maurice Norman, John White, Peter Baker, Jimmy Greaves, Ron Henry and Bill Nicholson with thumbs up.

Another trophy, another massive celebration down the High Road – but this one was a bit special. Heading the open-top bus are the "Tottenham Angels"

Left: Back in Europe after a three-year absence, Tottenham met AC Milan in the 1971/72 UEFA Cup semi-final. All the experience gained during the 1960s paid off, as Spurs beat one of the true giants of the game – Gianni Rivera, the *catenaccio* defensive system and all – 3-2 on aggregate. After Steve Perryman's two long-range efforts secured a 2-1 win in the home leg, Alan Mullery scored the vital away goal at the San Siro, with a thumping 20-yard drive that left Fabio Cudicini (father of modern-day Tottenham reserve keeper Carlo) well beaten.

Below: Mike England climbs high above the AC Milan defenders at White Hart Lane.

England does battle with Derek Dougan in the first leg of the 1972 UEFA Cup final at Molineux. Spurs won 2-1 thanks to a Chivers's brace, and followed it up with a 1-1 draw at home, a Mullery goal ensuring Spurs became the first British side to win two different European trophies.

Above: Spurs defended the UEFA Cup in season 1972/73, beating Red Star Belgrade 2-0 in November, before succumbing at the semi-final stage to Liverpool.

Right: Bill Nicholson with Dinamo Tbilisi coach Alexander Kotrekadze ahead of their sides' meeting at White Hart Lane in the UEFA Cup in December 1973 (Spurs won 5-1, 6-2 on aggregate). Europe was Bill Nick's natural home, with the emphasis on technique and tactical detail enabling his managerial acumen to flourish. This campaign was to end in disaster, however, with defeat in the final against Feyenoord overshadowed by rioting Spurs fans in Rotterdam, which in turn led to a European home game ban. It hit Nicholson hard and contributed to his resignation in September 1974.

Above: Returning to European competition after seven years, Spurs met Barcelona in an infamous Cup Winners' Cup semi-final clash in London. The Catalans resorted to disgraceful dirty tactics, and took a 1-0 lead after an uncharacteristic error from Spurs goalkeeper Ray Clemence. Garth Crooks (top left) had gone close, but it took a late equalizer from Graham Roberts (above) to draw Spurs level. It was all in vain, however, as Spurs lost 1-0 in the second leg.

Right: Roberts was in the thick of things again in November 1983, holding Bayern Munich to a 1-0 win at the Olympic Stadion. Spurs went through 2-1 on aggregate.

For many supporters the finest trophy-lifting European campaign was in 1983/84, when Spurs won the UEFA Cup for a second time. Meeting holders Anderlecht in the final, Spurs were missing key players through injury and suspension (Hoddle and Perryman among them), but with a battling display in both legs eventually won through 4-3 on penalties, after the teams were deadlocked at 2-2 on aggregate. In the main picture, Spurs players are about to rush and acclaim penalty-saving hero Tony Parks, whose famous save from Arnor Gudjohnsen (father of Eidur) sealed victory. Left to right in front of a delirious White Hart Lane crowd: Ossie Ardiles, Gary Stevens, Graham Roberts (who earlier scored Tottenham's vital equalizer) and Chris Hughton.

Hughton tussles with Enzo Scifo.

Seventies' Ups and Downs
1970-1979

Spurs players nervously await a Leeds United free-kick, during an FA Cup tie in January 1972.

1970 Tottenham Hotspur sign Martin Peters from West Ham for £200,000; Jimmy Greaves goes the other way, after nine years at White Hart Lane **1971** Spurs win the League Cup for the first time **1972** The away league game at Leeds United is played at Hull City's Boothferry Park – Elland Road was closed due to hooliganism **1972** Spurs win the UEFA Cup **1973** Tottenham win the League Cup for the second time **1974** Tottenham lose the UEFA Cup final and are banned from playing their next two home European games at White Hart Lane after serious crowd trouble **1974** After nearly 16 years as manager, Bill Nicholson resigns; Terry Neill appointed manager **1975** Spurs avoid relegation on the last day of the season with a 4-2 win over Leeds **1975** Glenn Hoddle makes his professional debut **1976** Neill resigns; Keith Burkinshaw appointed manager **1977** Tottenham finish bottom and are relegated after 27 years in the top flight **1977** Pat Jennings joins Arsenal **1978** Spurs promoted at the first attempt **1978** Argentinian World Cup winners Osvaldo Ardiles and Ricardo Villa join Tottenham: "Burkinshaw's £750,000 deal scoops the world" runs the *Daily Mirror* headline **1979** Tony Galvin, a £30,000 signing from non-league Goole Town makes his debut

Bill Nicholson talks to the Spurs squad during a training session in July 1971. Despite further trophy-winning success, Nicholson struggled to work in the different circumstances the decade presented. He was uncomfortable with growing demands from the media, the emergence of agents and increasing player power, and despaired of hooliganism. Spurs had changed, football had changed, and too much of that change was not to the great man's liking.

125

Spurs entered the new decade as one of the country's top sides and maintained their status with a series of cup wins. But in the league, it was a case of a steady decline, with the third place of 1970/71 the best finish during the 1970s. In September 1970, they beat Manchester City 2-0 (above) thanks to goals from the new main attack pair, Chivers and Gilzean.

Above Left: Alan Mullery took over the captaincy following the departure of Dave Mackay and led by resolute example. For the January 1971 meeting with Everton, he tosses a coin with England colleague Alan Ball, the former Blackpool midfielder wearing his distinctive white boots.

Above: Liverpool were beginning to emerge as the dominant force in the English game, but Spurs could still hold their own, handing out a 2-0 defeat to the Merseysiders in September 1971. Here, Ralph Coates challenges Ian Callaghan.

Left: One of the bright new stars at Spurs was Steve Perryman. He had made his debut at the age of just 17 in September 1969 and, by the time he took to the field for the 1-0 league win over Liverpool in October 1970, was already well established in the Tottenham midfield.

FOOTBALL -STATS-

Cyril Knowles

Name: Cyril Barry Knowles

Born: 1944

Died: 1991

Playing Career: 1963-1976

Clubs: Middlesbrough, Tottenham Hotspur

Tottenham Appearances: 505

Goals: 17

-LEGENDS-

Cyril Knowles

For all the fond nostalgia for the 1970s, in reality it was a period when commercialism and cynicism crept into the game. The sport was starting to lose its sense of fun, but if one player was still determined to play with a smile on his face, it was Cyril Knowles. In his 12 years of service to Spurs as one of the finest full-backs the club has ever had, his infectious enthusiasm endeared him to team-mates and supporters alike. It was thus little surprise that in 1973 he was immortalized in a hit record, *Nice One Cyril* by The Cockerel Chorus, who took the catchline from a TV ad of the day for bread and turned it into a jovial homage to the Tottenham left-back. Knowles was a superb ball-playing defender and enjoyed plenty of professional success, but lived a life with more than its fair share of tragedy. He lost his young son in a freak car accident and died from a brain tumour at the age of just 47 – a sad end to a terrace favourite still much loved at Spurs today.

–LEGENDS–

Martin Peters

Famously described by Alf Ramsey as a footballer "10 years ahead of his time", Martin Peters played more league games for both West Ham and Norwich, but ranks as a Spurs great in large part because he was such a natural Spurs player. Elegant, cultured and stylish, he was a dynamic attacking midfielder behind much of Tottenham's success in the first half of the 1970s. A World Cup winner and scorer in 1966, he earned 67 caps for England in total, and after retiring as a player returned to White Hart Lane as a director in 1998, a role which he served with typical application for four years.

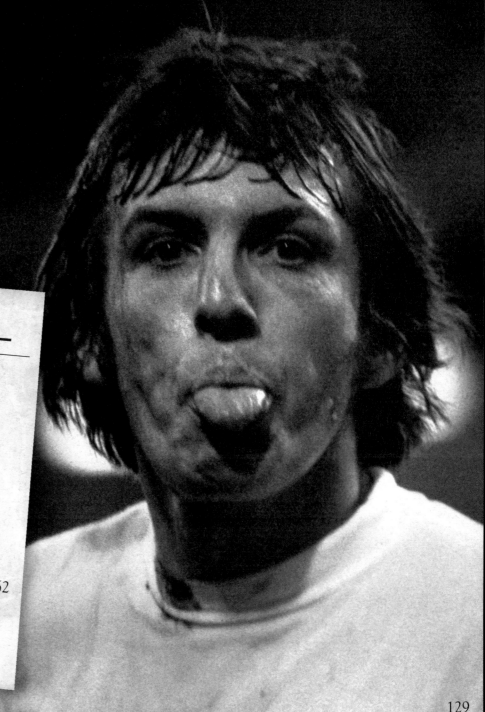

FOOTBALL –STATS–

Martin Peters

Name: Martin Stanford Peters MBE

Born: 1943

Playing Career: 1963-1981

Clubs: West Ham, Tottenham Hotspur, Norwich City, Sheffield United

Tottenham Appearances: 262

Goals: 76

Left: With attendances in general decline and a need to attract new fans, the traditionally male-dominated game was tentatively trying to appeal to women. In 1970 *Goal* magazine launched "Goal 70", a competition to find Britain's number one female supporter. The winner was Spurs fan Leslie Powell aged 18 from Woking. A hair stylist, she won "a crown, a football, and a cash prize of £100", and was pictured celebrating at the Waldorf Hotel in London.

Top Right: Club class . . . Top footballers were now firmly part of the jet set. On international duty for England's 1971 visit to Malta are Tottenham trio (left to right) Alan Mullery, Martin Chivers and Martin Peters.

Below Right: Tottenham and Arsenal players have often been friends off the pitch and north London hostilities abated for a more relaxed game of cricket between the two teams in July 1973. Offering his heartfelt commiserations to Charlie George is Phil Beal (right), straight after the Spurs defender had bowled the Arsenal striker out for a duck. The match was held to raise money for the local Woodberry Down Boys Club.

131

–LEGENDS–

Martin Chivers

Martin Harcourt Chivers had a distinctive name and a manner to match in his golden years at Spurs, his imposing, athletic frame helping to frighten defences for the seven years he spent in the Lilywhite shirt. With 174 goals in 355 games, Chivers ranks as the club's third greatest goalscorer and as the leading goalscorer in Europe with 22.

   At 6ft 1in, a shade under 14 stone, and no stranger to the White Hart Lane weights room, Chivers wielded raw power as an important weapon in his armoury but also more subtle qualities. Naturally balanced and possessing a fine first touch, he ably fulfilled the role of main Spurs striker so illustriously carried out by predecessors such as Greaves, Smith and Duquemin. His all-round talent was best encapsulated in the second of the two goals he scored in the first leg of the 1972 UEFA Cup final, winning the ball on the left-hand touchline, cutting inside and unleashing a venomous 35-yard drive.

Left: Alan Gilzean (far left) roars his approval as Chivers, in the famous number 9 shirt, takes the acclaim for his opener in a 2-0 extra-time win against Bristol City, in the 1971 League Cup semi-final second-leg match at White Hart Lane.

FOOTBALL
–STATS–

Martin Chivers

Name: Martin Harcourt Chivers

Born: 1945

Playing Career: 1962-1980

Clubs: Southampton, Tottenham Hotspur, Servette, Norwich City, Brighton

Tottenham Appearances: 355

Goals: 174

Tottenham repeated the League Cup-winning feat of 1971 two years later with a hard-earned 1-0 win against Norwich City.

Above: The faces tell their own story. Winning any trophy was always a cause for celebration, but there was little of the euphoria that had come in the preceding decade or so when there were more glittering prizes to parade. Tottenham's gradual removal from the top tier of British football continued, and a victory over modest opposition (Norwich finished third from bottom that season and were relegated the next) did not conceal the overall decline.

Right: Martin Peters shows his customary elegance on the ball.

Left: The happiest man at Wembley that March day in 1973 was Ralph Coates. The former Burnley player had struggled to justify the then club record fee of £190,000 when he had signed from Burnley two years before, but his goal was vindication of his worth to the side.

Below: Bill Nicholson and Martin Chivers had an occasionally difficult relationship, and the arguments over the striker's new contract in 1974 reportedly played a part in the manager's disenchantment with the modern game. Nonetheless, there was a mutual respect between the two, and they were happy to share in the club's cup success.

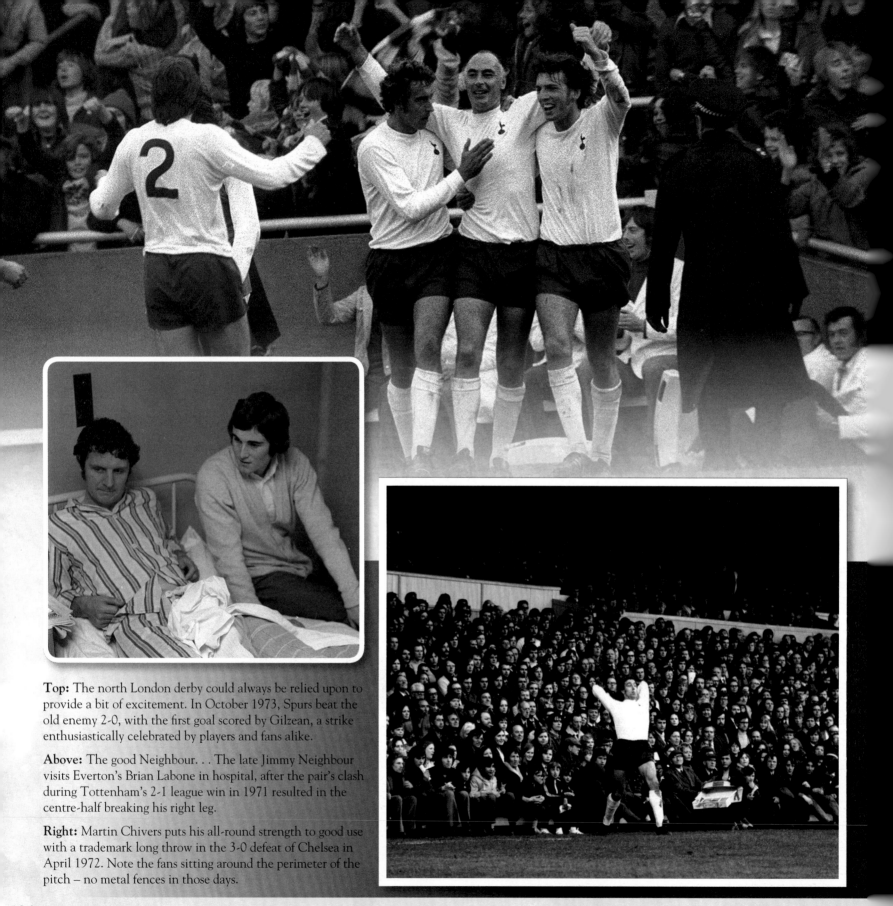

Top: The north London derby could always be relied upon to provide a bit of excitement. In October 1973, Spurs beat the old enemy 2-0, with the first goal scored by Gilzean, a strike enthusiastically celebrated by players and fans alike.

Above: The good Neighbour... The late Jimmy Neighbour visits Everton's Brian Labone in hospital, after the pair's clash during Tottenham's 2-1 league win in 1971 resulted in the centre-half breaking his right leg.

Right: Martin Chivers puts his all-round strength to good use with a trademark long throw in the 3-0 defeat of Chelsea in April 1972. Note the fans sitting around the perimeter of the pitch – no metal fences in those days.

In the battle of the combovers, Ralph Coates holds off Manchester United's Bobby Charlton in March 1973.

Bottom Left: Tottenham were a regular choice for the TV cameras. The proximity of White Hart Lane to London studios no doubt helped, but the club's culture of entertaining football was always a big draw. In regulation sheepskin jacket, commentator Barry Davies braves the attention of the White Hart Lane crowd before the 1973 League Cup semi-final against Wolves.

Bottom Right: No banks of flat screen plasma TVs or computerized, super slo-mo gizmos in sight: just a BBC commentator and an unruffled member of the off-camera staff in the Beeb's production suite.

Trouble on the Terraces

Football violence was an almost unavoidable feature of the sport during the 1970s. Hooligan gangs began to rise in profile, and fights on the terraces, pitch invasions and serious disorder became depressingly regular occurrences. Unfortunately, White Hart Lane did not escape trouble, with the London derby against Chelsea at Tottenham in April 1975 an infamous example.

With both sides battling against relegation, tensions were already high. Sporadic trouble both inside and outside the ground culminated in a pitch invasion and brawl that forced referee Jack Taylor to delay the start, and bravely try to usher fans off the pitch. Fortunately order was restored and the game was played, with Spurs winning 2-0 thanks to goals from Alfie Conn and Steve Perryman. For innocent fans caught up in the melee however, particularly youngsters, football grounds were becoming increasingly risky and frightening places to visit.

The mid-1970s was a grim time for Spurs, but Alfie Conn provided some of the happier moments. Bill Nick's last signing, he arrived from Rangers with a £140,000 price tag hanging around his neck, and only featured in 38 games for Tottenham in a three-year period. Yet, with his rock star looks and off-the-cuff style he became a cult figure to supporters, and was instrumental in the dramatic last-day 4-2 win over Leeds that preserved Tottenham's Division One status in 1975. Here, he is losing his right boot in shooting for goal against Norwich in 1976.

Below: A proud moment for Perryman as he presents the FA Cup in the 1981 victory parade.

Inset: Small in stature, Perryman was a combative presence in midfield and attack, as in this tussle with Nottingham Forest's Bob Chapman in 1975.

FOOTBALL
–STATS–

Steve Perryman

Name: Steven John Perryman MBE

Born: 1951

Playing Career: 1969-1990

Clubs: Tottenham Hotspur, Oxford, Brentford

Tottenham Appearances: 854

Goals: 39

–LEGENDS–

Steve Perryman

Over 850 games speak for themselves. In a Spurs career that spanned three decades, Steve Perryman made a record number of appearances for Tottenham, displaying a level of loyalty and devotion to the cause that few other clubs have been privileged to enjoy.

From the day he first walked into White Hart Lane as a much-coveted 17-year-old, Perryman placed his faith in Spurs, politely declining the advances of a number of other outfits in the belief that Tottenham would be the best club to nurture, improve and reward his talent. Despite the odd setback, notably relegation in 1977, and reported continuing interest from more successful sides, Perryman kept his side of the bargain, skippering the team back to the top flight and on to cup glory. It reflected his own high standards of duty and sense of "doing the right thing": Perryman shouldered his share of responsibility for the drop, and dedicated himself to paying back the trust and faith the fans had showed the players. What helped in realizing that aim is something that is occasionally overlooked when evaluating his worth to the club: Steve Perryman was also an outstanding footballer.

Perryman's loyalty is a rare attribute that abides to this day, over 20 years since he kicked his last ball for the club. At supporter functions and charity events, he devotes hours of his time to speaking to the fans, sharing his memories and talking with fondness about the club he loves. If there is one player who most obviously understands what it means to be a Tottenham fan, and in doing so provides a link to the ethos of the Bill Nicholson era, it is Steve Perryman.

143

The Relegation Years

The mid-1970s was a miserable period for Tottenham, with the team engaged in relegation struggles and distracted by off-the-pitch upheaval. Terry Neill (right, with Perryman) arrived as Bill Nick's replacement, but it was a doomed relationship. Neill staved off the drop in his first season and achieved mid-table respectability the next, but in the midst of rows with the board and rancour with supporters who could never quite accept him for his Arsenal connections, nor understand why Danny Blanchflower had not got the job, Neill resigned at the end of the 1976/77 season and headed off to Highbury.

Above: In the middle of a tense season, players were almost bound to succumb to the pressure and in the north London derby of December 1976, a punch-up predictably ensued. Here, defender Willie Young (5) and Arsenal keeper Jimmy Rimmer are held apart by a linesman as tempers fray during the 2-2 draw at White Hart Lane. Young scored but was soon having to make peace with his opponents: he left Spurs in March 1977 and followed Terry Neill to the home of Tottenham's arch rivals.

Right: February 1975 and Martin Peters cuts a dejected figure playing for Spurs Reserves against their Birmingham counterparts at a deserted White Hart Lane. That one of England's best strikers was banished to the "stiffs" sums up the general unease and drift that plagued the club during this sorry period. (Note the boards in alphabetical order around the perimeter of the pitch. These were used to update supporters on games taking place around the country. Each letter corresponded to a particular fixture as detailed in the programme.)

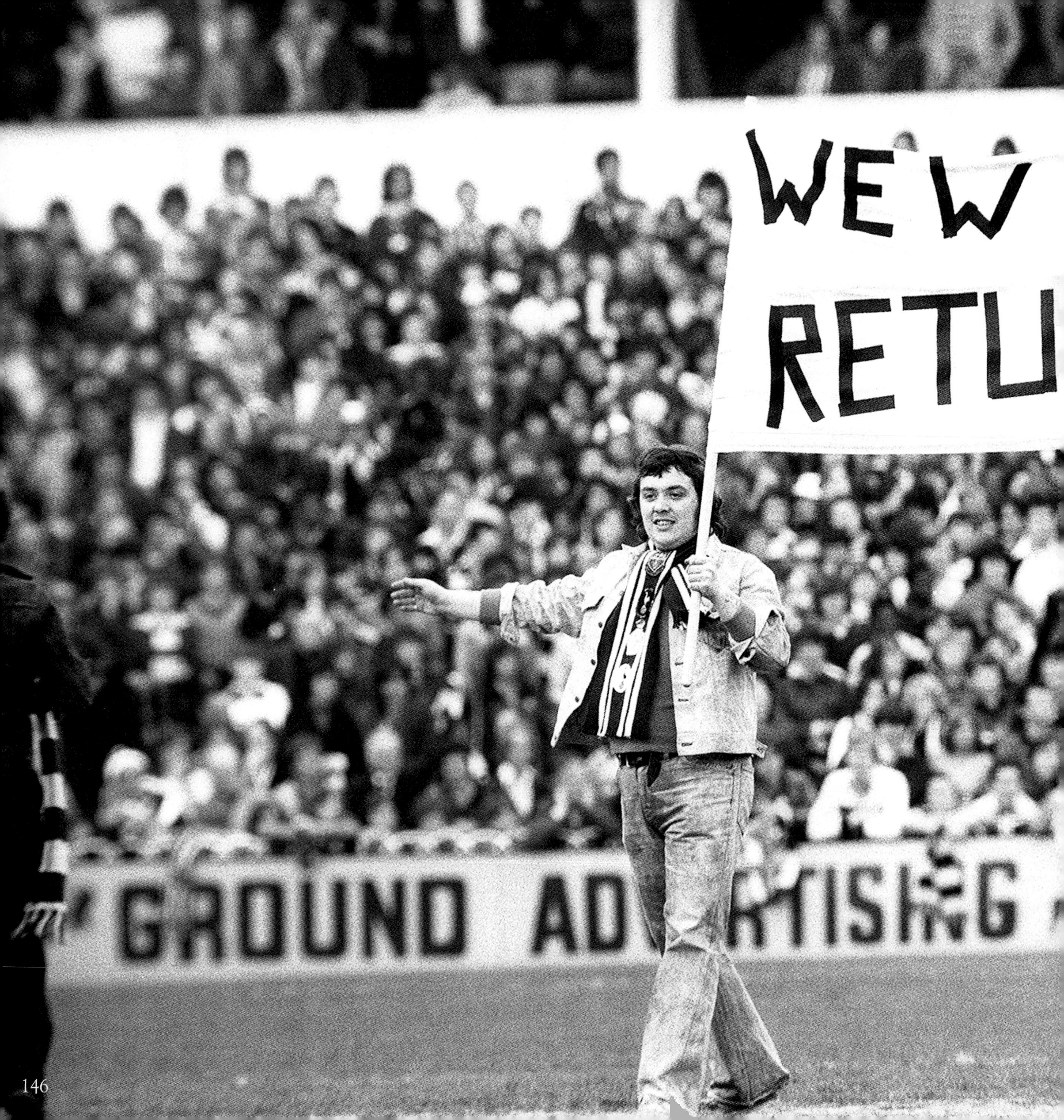
WE W
RETU
GROUND ADV RTISING

14ᵗʰ May 1977. On the day of relegation reckoning, Spurs fans show their defiance. The end had effectively come with a 5-0 defeat at Manchester City a week earlier, making the 2-0 win over Leicester City in the final home game an academic case of too little too late. But over 26,000 were there to bid Tottenham farewell, a healthy attendance at the time, and an indication that Tottenham's supporters would stay loyal to the cause. They did in huge numbers: the home crowd average actually rose by over 10% the next season.

The spell in Division Two was a brief but productive one. Spurs made an immediate return, coming up on goal difference ahead of Brighton after a final day goalless draw with fellow promotion-winners Southampton. The period out of the top flight was just what Spurs needed, enabling the club to regroup and develop exciting new players like Glenn Hoddle, pictured on the left with Peter Taylor and Barry Daines (right).

Above: Ardiles and Villa arrive at Gatwick Airport, the start of a long love affair with Spurs.

Top: *Muy bueno* . . . Fresh from celebrating promotion, Tottenham pulled off one of the greatest transfer coups in football history with an audacious double-swoop for Ossie Ardiles and Ricky Villa. The transfer stunned the country. A generation before the Premier League, foreign superstars were alien to the British game, but with a mould-breaking attitude that typified the club, Spurs led the way in signing talent from around the world. Here Ardiles and Villa are greeted by ecstatic fans on 17th July 1978.

Right: At home with the Ardiles and Villa families. Ossie, Ricky and their families settle down to life in Britain.

FOOTBALL
–STATS–

Ossie Ardiles

Name: Osvaldo Cesar Ardiles

Born: 1952

Playing Career: 1973-1991

Clubs: Instituto Cordoba, Belgrano, Huracan, Tottenham Hotspur, Blackburn Rovers, QPR, Swindon Town

Tottenham Appearances: 293

Goals: 25

"My ambition is to have a very good season, win the league and play at Wembley," said Ardiles when he joined Spurs in July 1978. The league title eluded him, but his Wembley dream became a reality.

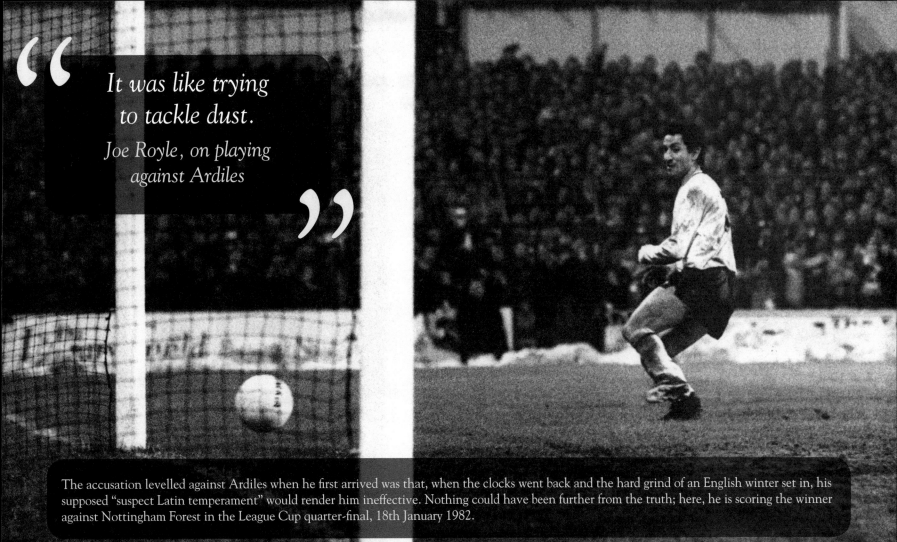

> ❝ *It was like trying to tackle dust.*
>
> *Joe Royle, on playing against Ardiles* ❞

The accusation levelled against Ardiles when he first arrived was that, when the clocks went back and the hard grind of an English winter set in, his supposed "suspect Latin temperament" would render him ineffective. Nothing could have been further from the truth; here, he is scoring the winner against Nottingham Forest in the League Cup quarter-final, 18th January 1982.

–LEGENDS–

Ossie Ardiles

Few foreign players have had such a dramatic and lasting impact on the British game as Ossie Ardiles. Eric Cantona, Thierry Henry, Peter Schmeichel and others may have won more trophies, but they and all modern imports owe a debt of gratitude to the little Argentinean who, along with compatriot Ricky Villa, paved the way for outsiders to play and thrive in the hurly-burly of the English game.

Ardiles was a brilliant midfielder, who combined typical South American flair with a work rate that put many of his adopted countrymen to shame. The sight of Ardiles buzzing around the pitch, playing devastatingly simple short passes or embarking on one of his mazy dribbles, with the ball seemingly tied to his feet, is one of the most cherished images Spurs fans have of the late 1970s and 1980s. Allied to his footballing skills were his qualities as a character: perceptive, intelligent and witty, he was immensely popular with team-mates and supporters, and even his failures as Spurs manager did nothing to dull the esteem he is held in by the Tottenham faithful.

Spurs Are on their Way to Wembley
1980-1989

Tottenham are back: Ricky Villa has just scored the greatest ever FA Cup final goal and the wild celebrations begin, 14th May 1981.
Spurs players in white, left to right: Ossie Ardiles, Chris Hughton, Villa, Garth Crooks.

1980 Tottenham Hotspur sign strikers Steve Archibald and Garth Crooks for a combined £1.45m 1981 Spurs win the FA Cup for the sixth time 1982 Defeat to Liverpool in the League Cup final is Tottenham's first loss in a major final at Wembley 1982 Spurs win the FA Cup for the second consecutive year 1982 The new West Stand is officially opened 1983 Holsten become Tottenham's first shirt sponsor 1983 Tottenham become the first football club to be listed on the Stock Exchange, raising £3.8m in new capital; Irving Scholar becomes chairman 1984 Tottenham win the UEFA Cup in Keith Burkinshaw's last game in charge 1984 Peter Shreeve appointed manager 1985 Spurs finish third in Division One, their highest position for 14 years 1986 Shreeve sacked, David Pleat becomes manager 1987 Tottenham lose an FA Cup final for the first time, finish third in the league and are knocked out in the dying minutes of the League Cup semi-final replay by Arsenal 1988 Pleat sacked, Terry Venables becomes manager 1988 Paul Gascoigne signs for a record British fee of £2m 1989 The first ever televised live league game ends with a 3-2 home defeat for Spurs by Nottingham Forest 1989 Gary Lineker makes his debut for Spurs

Villa and Crooks show off the FA Cup to a section of the vast crowd that welcomed the players home to London N17 in 1981.

For the first couple of seasons back in the top flight it was a matter of consolidation for Spurs as new players settled and others adjusted to the more testing rigours of Division One. The FA Cup provided a foretaste of things to come with two exciting Cup runs between 1978 and 1980, both ending at the quarter-final stage to Manchester United and Liverpool respectively.

Background: Getting a bird's-eye view of the action was a fireman on an extended ladder high above the West Stand roof.

Top Right: Chris Hughton receives attention from physio Mike Varney. Note the perimeter fences.

Below: Two weeks after the mighty Liverpool had dashed Tottenham's hopes in the Cup, Spurs exacted revenge on the champions with a daring 2-0 home win in the league – daring because Keith Burkinshaw opted for a risky 4-2-4 formation to take the game to the Merseysiders. Future Spurs keeper Ray Clemence looks anguished as Spurs celebrate John Pratt's goal.

Bottom Right: In what was a bruising encounter, Spurs refused to be cowed by Liverpool's physical tactics, but they picked up several injuries for their troubles. Here, popular defender Terry Naylor provides more work for Varney.

By 1980, Burkinshaw's team were settled and ready to take a tilt at the honours. The manager had promised to construct a winning side, and was about to see his ambition realized.

Above: Steve Archibald, signed from Aberdeen for £850,000, forged a lethal and productive partnership with Garth Crooks. Here's the Scotsman eluding Kenny Burns in the 2-0 win over then European Cup-holders Nottingham Forest in August 1980.

Right: Ossie Ardiles had established himself in the Spurs midfield and proved his doubters wrong. Here, he takes on Arsenal's Liam Brady.

Right: The brightest talent in the emerging Spurs side was Glenn Hoddle. By now an England regular, he was turning in exceptional performances on a consistent basis. With typical athleticism, he drives the ball home in the 3-1 FA Cup third-round replay victory over QPR, leaving future West Ham and Newcastle boss Glenn Roeder helpless. The Cup run was under way.

Below: Tony Galvin, the Russian Studies graduate and left-winger signed from non-league Goole Town, proved to be a shrewd acquisition by Burkinshaw. Here is Galvin in action during the 2-0 defeat of eventual champions Aston Villa in March 1981.

After a 1981 FA Cup run in which they had to leave London only once for the semi-final against Wolves, Spurs headed for Wembley as favourites to beat Manchester City. Unfortunately, City's uncompromising tactics disrupted Tottenham's usual fluent style, and with 10 minutes of normal time remaining, Spurs were lucky to draw level, force extra time and then a replay after Tommy Hutchinson deflected a Hoddle free-kick into City's net.

Left: Several Tottenham players, including Graham Roberts, went down with cramp in extra time, exhausted by the humidity and 120 minutes of hard graft on Wembley's wide open spaces. The tough centre-half also picked up a nasty injury, after an accidental clash with team-mate Chris Hughton left Roberts missing two teeth.

Below: Chief among Tottenham's tormentors was Gerry Gow whose near-the-knuckle tackling did much to upset Spurs' midfield rhythm.

Left: At the final whistle Hughton, Ardiles and Paul Miller head for a well-earned rest. In the background is a disconsolate Ricky Villa, subbed midway through the second half after an ineffectual display and his confidence shattered. Within seconds of this picture being taken, however, his mood lifted. With a stroke of man-management genius, Burkinshaw announced in the dressing room in front of the whole team, "Ricky, you're playing in the replay".

Below: Relief for Hoddle and substitute Garry Brooke.

Below: Spurs fans were out in force and in vociferous mood for their first trip to Wembley in eight years.

Left: The build-up to the 1981 FA Cup final replay was a much more relaxed affair for Spurs than in the first game. With less of the pomp and ceremony of Saturday's match, Tottenham could focus on a Thursday evening game, which was to be Steve Perryman's 599th for the club, and with the bulk of the crowd rooting for Spurs.

Right: All Graham Roberts wanted for Christmas was his missing front tooth.

Far Right: It would never have happened in Jimmy Dimmock's day . . . With glamour shots now a mainstay of the tabloids, the pre-match build-up included some soft-focus pictures of female supporters. Shelly Keston (daughter of legendary fan Morris Keston and at the time engaged to defender Paul Miller) shows her allegiances.

Below Right: Garth Crooks sees what it's like to be on the other side of the striker–goalkeeper battle.

Below: Hoddle with his eyes on the prize.

163

Left: A notable feature of the 1981 replay was how many more Spurs fans were at the game than City supporters. Tottenham fans began queuing for tickets at Wembley immediately after the first game ended and then swarmed to a rainy White Hart Lane on Monday to snap up the rest. With the recession biting hard and facing another expensive trip to London, many City fans opted to stay at home and watch on TV, leaving hordes of Tottenham fans to take their places on the terraces.

Above: Spurs fan Dale Mitchell, with hair dyed blue and white, was one of the thousands who queued for up to 16 hours.

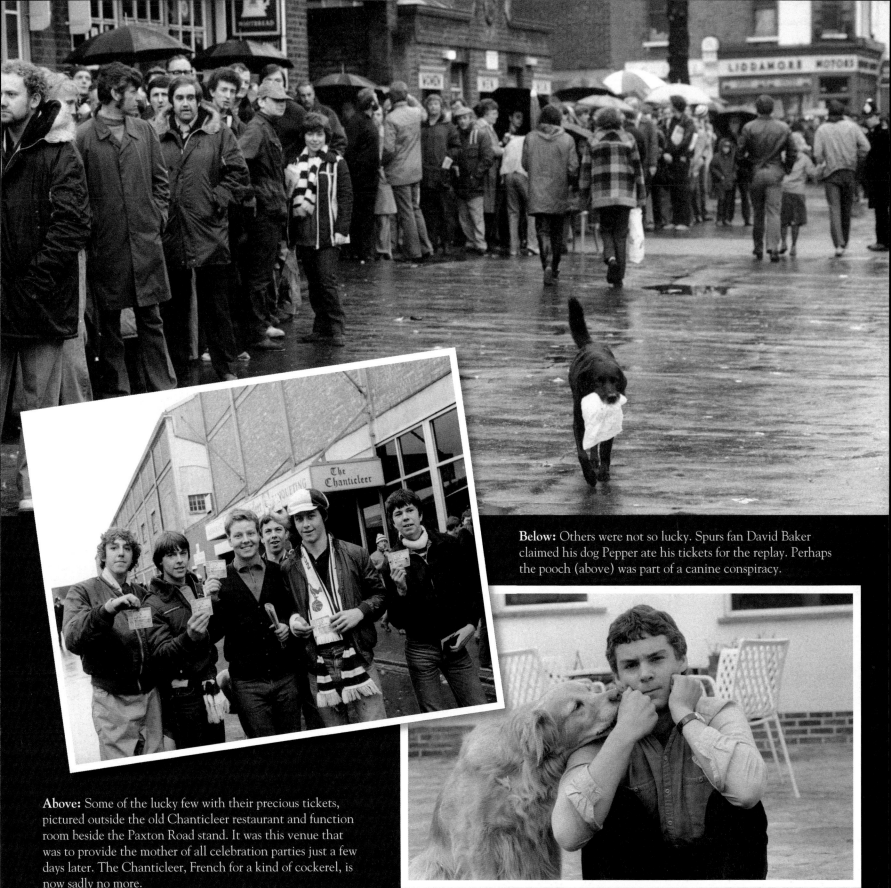

Below: Others were not so lucky. Spurs fan David Baker claimed his dog Pepper ate his tickets for the replay. Perhaps the pooch (above) was part of a canine conspiracy.

Above: Some of the lucky few with their precious tickets, pictured outside the old Chanticleer restaurant and function room beside the Paxton Road stand. It was this venue that was to provide the mother of all celebration parties just a few days later. The Chanticleer, French for a kind of cockerel, is now sadly no more.

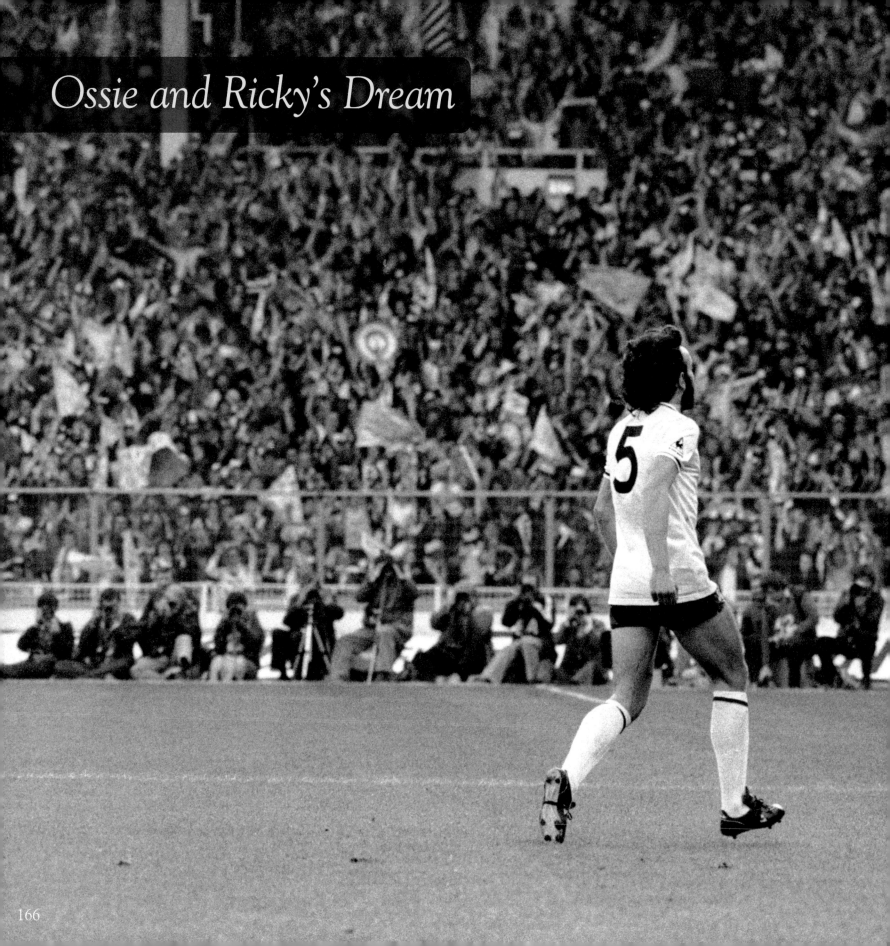

Left: Ricky Villa celebrates scoring the opening goal in the 1981 FA Cup final replay, with the massed ranks of delirious Tottenham fans in front of him.

Below: For the replay, Ossie Ardiles and his team-mates refused to be intimidated by Gow, and dominated the midfield as a result.

The Greatest Goal in FA Cup Final History

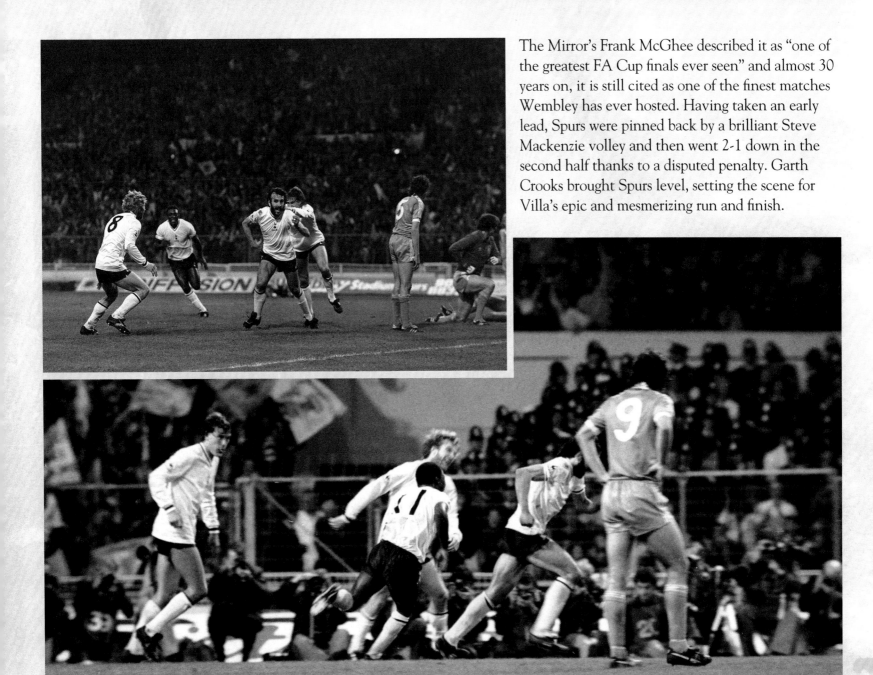

The Mirror's Frank McGhee described it as "one of the greatest FA Cup finals ever seen" and almost 30 years on, it is still cited as one of the finest matches Wembley has ever hosted. Having taken an early lead, Spurs were pinned back by a brilliant Steve Mackenzie volley and then went 2-1 down in the second half thanks to a disputed penalty. Garth Crooks brought Spurs level, setting the scene for Villa's epic and mesmerizing run and finish.

> " Above all I am thrilled for the fans who have waited a long time for success and now they have their pride back. They did not desert us when we slipped into the Second Division. I hope we have repaid them for their loyalty. "
>
> Keith Burkinshaw

–LEGENDS–

Glenn Hoddle

The greatest creative midfielder of his generation, it was perhaps Glenn Hoddle's misfortune to play in an era when English football relied largely on defensive, physical tactics and was not the multi-billion pound leisure industry it is today. Had Hoddle been a player in the modern age, his talent would have flourished to an even greater degree and his fame would have been phenomenal.

Underappreciated by many in the domestic game, Hoddle was adored by Spurs fans. His perfect balance, powerful shot, brilliance at set pieces and sublime artistry made him a hero to his supporters standing on the Shelf or the Park Lane. Above all it was his passing that made him so special, with an ability to execute raking, inch-perfect deliveries under even the tightest marking.

The lynchpin of Burkinshaw's promotion side and cup-winning teams, Hoddle won 53 England caps but should have won many more. That national team managers chose to build their teams around the more physical qualities of the injury-prone Bryan Robson played its part in the team's underachievement; as Michel Platini said of Hoddle, "if he was French he would have won 150 caps".

After 12 years as a Spurs player, Hoddle returned to White Hart Lane as manager in 2001 in difficult circumstances, at a time when Tottenham were struggling to regain their position as one of the country's biggest clubs. Despite ultimately failing to deliver, Hoddle's reputation with the fans did not suffer. He was, and remains, the King of White Hart Lane.

> " *Hoddle a luxury? It's the bad players who are a luxury.*
> Danny Blanchflower "

Long before David Beckham, Hoddle was a fashion-conscious icon, as seen here sporting a then very trendy Pringle jumper.

A youthful Hoddle proudly shows off his car in 1976.

Eight years later, and pictured with his then wife Anne, Hoddle had graduated to a sponsored Saab 900 Turbo, complete with gifts and products he had received and been asked to endorse.

The Grand Parade

With the club starved of success for so long, if anything the victory parade crowds in the 1980s were even bigger than during the 1960s. Upwards of 250,000 people packed the High Road, from the Angel, Edmonton, to Tottenham Town Hall, to greet the team home on Sunday 17th May 1981.

Bottom Far Left: Every vantage point was used.

Left: The morning after the night before: famous *Daily Mirror* photographer Monte Fresco couldn't resist sharing in the glory with Garth Crooks.

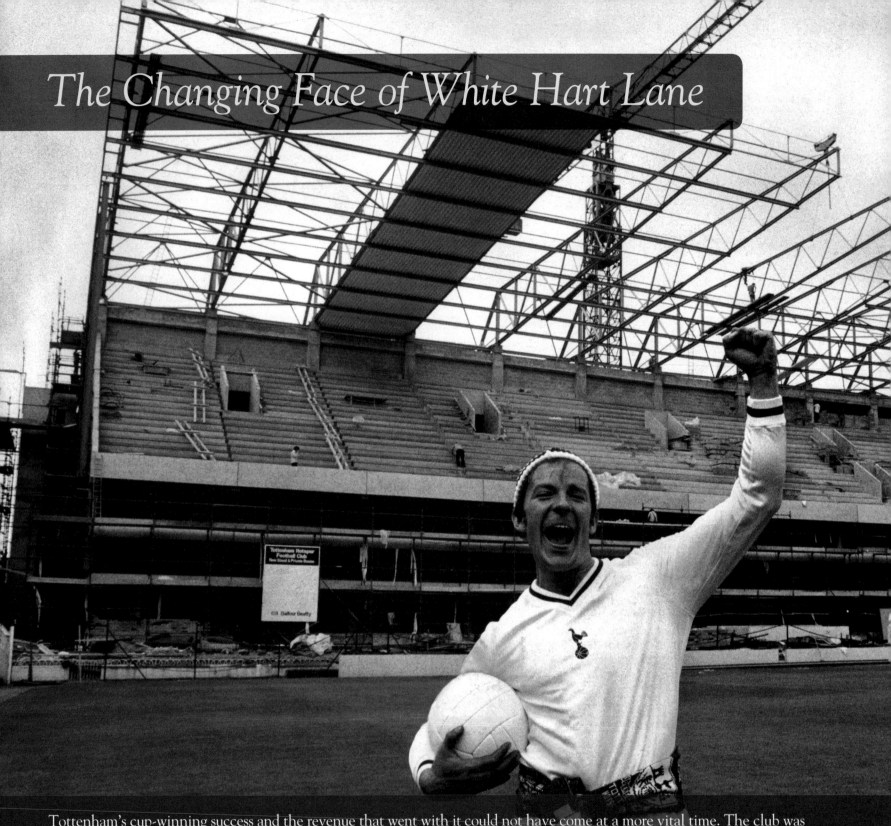

The Changing Face of White Hart Lane

Tottenham's cup-winning success and the revenue that went with it could not have come at a more vital time. The club was committed to an expensive £3.25 million rebuild of the West Stand that ultimately cost £5m, the first stage of a programme that promised to completely modernize White Hart Lane. The new stadium was eventually finished by the late 1990s, but not without controversy, and on two occasions the development pushed Spurs into severe debt and towards the financial brink.

Left: Mick Crompton, a Tottenham fan and one of the roofer "monkeys" who built the 70ft-high cantilevered roof of the new West Stand.

Top Right: The complete West Stand may have looked impressive, but with a capacity of 6,500 was too small considering its cost.

Middle Right: Former chairman Irving Scholar and then manager Terry Venables present an artist's impression of the new White Hart Lane. It was a bold vision but one that was only partially realized.

Bottom Right: The most contentious redevelopment was that of the East Stand in 1988. Cost overruns forced the club into debt and prompted Alan Sugar's purchase of the club, while a delay in completion meant a safety certificate was not issued and the opening home game of the 1988/89 season had to be postponed. Worst of all was the loss of the beloved Shelf, the finest terraced view in the country – now but a fading memory.

That Winning Feeling

The period from 1981 to 1984 was a great time to be a Tottenham fan. It was the club's second most successful period, as the FA Cup was won twice, the UEFA Cup won in 1984, the League Cup was only narrowly lost in 1982 and there were, for the first time since the 1960s, realistic challenges for the title.

Far Left: Spurs were attempting an unprecedented quadruple in 1981/82, but with a fixture backlog and too small a squad, the number of matches caught up with them. Coupled with an exciting but risky playing style, the team were simply not equipped to land the title – unlike Everton, who twice pipped Spurs to the Championship during the decade. Here, in January 1982, Garth Crooks is foiled at Goodison Park. Note the criss-cross detail of the stand fascia in the background, a trademark of the architect Archibald Leitch who also designed the old White Hart Lane.

Left and Below: Compensation for missing out on other prizes came with the FA Cup in 1982. Spurs travelled to Chelsea for a London grudge match in March but were just too good for the Division Two side, winning 3-2 and sending the away fans into a frenzy.

If it's an FA Cup final, it must mean another Tottenham Hotspur FA Cup final song …. After the success of 'Ossie's Dream' the previous year, which had reached an impressive number 5 in the charts, the Spurs squad rejoined forces with cockney rockers Chas 'n' Dave to record 'Tottenham Tottenham' for the forthcoming final against QPR.

Ricky Villa and Glenn Hoddle are all smiles, but new goalkeeper Ray Clemence looks as if he'd be happier back between the sticks.

Hoddle gives divine thanks and is congratulated by Garth Crooks as the midfielder opens the scoring in the 1982 Cup final. A determined QPR soon pulled level, however, and forced another replay. Hoddle proved to be decisive in that game, scoring the only goal from the penalty spot (inset) to give Spurs their seventh FA Cup win, albeit with what may have been their most underwhelming FA Cup final performance.

–LEGENDS–

Graham Roberts

What would Tottenham give to have a player like Graham Roberts in their ranks now? Back in 1980, they paid out £35,000 to bring him from non-league Weymouth – a bargain then, and an absolute steal by today's standards. For "Robbo" was the dynamic, tough, uncompromising and never-say-die warrior all successful sides must have. He passed into legend for dumping Arsenal's Charlie Nicholas in the Highbury East Stand in 1986 and almost single-handedly earned his side extra time in the 1984 UEFA Cup final. Though he was also a fine footballer, it was his commitment to the Spurs cause that made him so popular. Other defenders such as Mike England, Paul Miller, Phil Beal and Maurice Norman played more games for Spurs, but few could match Roberts for heart-on-the-sleeve determination.

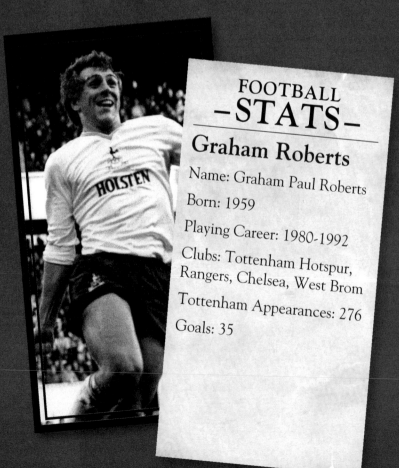

FOOTBALL –STATS–

Graham Roberts

Name: Graham Paul Roberts

Born: 1959

Playing Career: 1980-1992

Clubs: Tottenham Hotspur, Rangers, Chelsea, West Brom

Tottenham Appearances: 276

Goals: 35

–LEGENDS–

Chris Hughton

Chris Hughton, along with the likes of Tony Galvin, Paul Miller and Mark Falco, is one of the lesser-celebrated heroes of the 1980s' Tottenham side, but like them his relatively low profile has not disguised his true worth and service to the club.

As a successful home-grown player he was always likely to be popular with supporters, and as one of the first black footballers to become established at a major club, something of a pioneer. Living up to Tottenham's proud tradition of attacking full-backs, he was tenacious in the tackle, consistent, hard working, and able to rapidly spring into attack. He and Galvin formed an impressive partnership on the left flank that was an important facet of Tottenham's success during this period.

Hughton became a coach, assistant manager and an occasional caretaker during what was a time of considerable upheaval in recent years at Spurs, before he left for an even more tumultuous spell at Newcastle. Through it all he was a diligent and characteristically reliable presence, a true gentleman on and off the pitch.

FOOTBALL –STATS–

Chris Hughton

Name: Christopher William Gerard Hughton

Born: 1958

Playing Career: 1979-1993

Clubs: Tottenham Hotspur, West Ham, Brentford

Tottenham Appearances: 389

Goals: 19

Hughton rivalled Ossie Ardiles as one of the most popular members of the side among team-mates.

In an echo of the misfortune that befell the Double side, Spurs lost players at crucial times during the 1980s. Most sorely missed were Ardiles and Villa, who both had to sit out the 1982 FA Cup final in the midst of the Falklands War – it was felt political sensitivities were too acute for the Argentineans to play. Ardiles made his comeback in January 1983, playing for the reserves in front of an underwhelmed crowd at Luton.

Left: Ray Clemence proved to be a shrewd buy, the England international and former Liverpool favourite adding experience and composure to the Tottenham rearguard for 330 games.

Below: Joining Sir Alf Ramsey for Bill Nicholson's 1983 testimonial was Jimmy Greaves.

> "There used to be a football club over there.
>
> *Keith Burkinshaw*

Keith Burkinshaw bids a wistful farewell just before his final game, the UEFA Cup final second leg, 23rd May 1984.

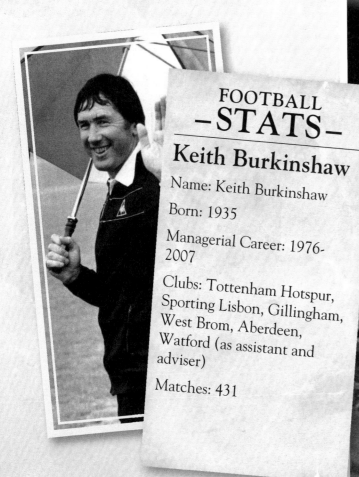

FOOTBALL
-STATS-
Keith Burkinshaw

Name: Keith Burkinshaw

Born: 1935

Managerial Career: 1976-2007

Clubs: Tottenham Hotspur, Sporting Lisbon, Gillingham, West Brom, Aberdeen, Watford (as assistant and adviser)

Matches: 431

-LEGENDS-

Keith Burkinshaw

Like Tottenham's greatest manager Bill Nicholson, the club's second most successful boss, Keith Burkinshaw, was fashioned from no-nonsense Yorkshire grit. Exacting in his standards and single-minded in how he felt a football club should be managed, he was nonetheless a true romantic: innovative, imaginative, and committed to the Spurs ethos of playing the game with style.

A dignified presence for eight years at White Hart Lane, like many successful managers he had only a modest playing career, with a brief spell at Liverpool and long service in the lower divisions with Workington and Scunthorpe. It was at Spurs he found his vocation, however, first as coach and then rebuilding the club in the post-Nicholson years to steer it to success at home and abroad. Unhappy with the business-orientated direction the club was taking under chairman Irving Scholar and with his power being diluted, he left with regrets but on a cup-winning high note. Having just secured the UEFA Cup in 1984 he walked out past the gates, supposedly uttering a lament about what Spurs had been and had become. Whether he did say it or not, the sentiment was a poignant one, eloquently expressing a great deal, not just about Spurs but about football in general.

New Faces, Familiar Near Misses'

Left: With Peter Shreeve now in charge, Spurs welcomed new signing Clive Allen (bottom), son of Les, to the attack, joined in training by Mark Falco and Gary Mabbutt.

Above: Chris Waddle was another welcome and successful addition, even with his mullet hairstyle.

Below: John Chiedozie was a popular winger who, in his unlikely post-playing career, became one of the country's leading suppliers of inflatable bouncy castles.

Above: Tottenham went to the top of the table with a 2-1 win at Highbury in January 1985, but form fell away and Shreeve's side finished a disappointing though ultimately creditable third. While Hoddle looks on bemusedly, a policeman pursues a fan who had run on to the pitch.

Right: A 1-0 win in March 1986 over the old enemy was greeted with typical joy by a crowd of 33,427, but the figure disguised a more general and worrying decline in attendances during the middle of the decade. Spurs did not avoid the slump: a risible 9,359 came through the turnstiles to see the 2-0 defeat of Birmingham City three weeks later.

Left: Hoddle shows he could put his foot in when required, with this crunching challenge on England team-mate Terry Butcher.

Above: Yes, that really is Diego Maradona in a Spurs shirt. The world's then greatest player lined up for Tottenham in Ossie Ardiles's 1986 testimonial against Inter Milan, just weeks before the World Cup.

Right: The hands of Hod welcome Maradona to White Hart Lane

Below: Though he gave Tottenham their highest league placing for 14 years, Shreeve lasted just one more season. Disenchanted with the way football was going, supporters were perhaps less patient, and quicker to voice their discontent, as with this impromptu demonstration on the High Road after a run of poor results in 1986.

191

The Nearly Season

Shreeve's replacement was David Pleat, who will for ever be remembered as the Spurs boss who almost cracked it. Despite a difficult start behind the scenes during which he clashed with several among the old guard in the squad, Pleat fashioned a team that were easy on the eye and at times unstoppable, the then groundbreaking 4–5–1 formation enabling striker Clive Allen to score a club record 49 goals in all competitions. As late as March, Spurs were in the running for all three domestic trophies (there was no European football after the ban on English teams prompted by the Heysel disaster), but with a crippling fixture list and injuries taking their toll, the side ran out of steam and finished the campaign empty-handed.

Clive Allen dresses in retro kit to mark the 100th derby between Spurs and Arsenal in January 1987. The reminder of a past when the Gunners seemed to confound Spurs, as in the 1919 promotion scandal, was apt: Arsenal beat Spurs in a tumultuous League Cup, three-game semi-final saga in which the exiled South Londoners took the lead for the first time with just one minute of normal time remaining in the replay.

Chris Waddle, perhaps the outstanding player that amazing season, celebrates goal number 23 of Clive Allen's remarkable 49-goal haul, as Spurs beat Chelsea 2-0 in December 1986.

In the FA Cup quarter-final at Wimbledon, Hoddle has just scored with an incredible free kick, and Waddle can't quite believe how good his team-mate is.

Back in the studio with Chas 'n' Dave, the squad record 'Hotshot Tottenham' for the forthcoming FA Cup final. The jaunty ditty was dedicated to Danny Thomas, whose career had been ended a month earlier by a dreadful tackle from QPR's Gavin Maguire. Chris Waddle might look as if he is lacking enthusiasm but he was soon back in the charts with a

A famous goal in one of Wembley's finest finals, but it meant misery for Spurs. Keith Houchen scores for Coventry with a diving header, and all Chris Hughton can do is watch and wail as the underdogs draw level and

Diamond Geezers

They carved out a brilliant partnership on the pitch and followed suit as a singing duo. Well, almost. Glenn Hoddle and Chris Waddle enjoyed a brief but glittering recording career in 1987, performing as the imaginatively named "Glenn and Chris". They reached a very respectable number 12 on 18th April with 'Diamond Lights' and even appeared on *Top of the Pops*, but the follow-up, 'It's Goodbye', was accurately named as it failed to make a mark and prompted a swift end to the music-making exploits of what could have been football's Lennon and McCartney.

Waddle, now minus the mullet, and Hoddle pose for publicity photos.

El Tel's Homecoming

After worsening results and scandal surrounding his private life, David Pleat was shown the door in 1987. There was, in truth, only one candidate to replace him: Terry Venables. The highly regarded manager and former Spurs player was back from Barcelona and looking to take Tottenham on to the promised land. Here he is in November 1987 with right-hand man Allan Harris (brother of Ron).

Venables rang the changes quickly. First of the big names to arrive was Paul Gascoigne for a British record £2m, along with Paul Stewart, signed from Manchester City for £1.4m . . .

. . . followed in June 1989 by arguably the most famous British footballer of the day, Gary Lineker, who followed Venables back on the homecoming trail from Catalonia. Sadly, Chris Waddle's enforced sale to Marseilles just a few weeks later hinted at the growing financial problems that were to plague Venables's tenure.

The Football Business
1990-1994

It all ended in tears . . . The laughter and smiles may have been genuine as directors, manager and players celebrate another FA Cup triumph with mini-trophy presentations to Lineker and Gascoigne, but the apparent harmony disguised major trouble brewing at White Hart Lane. Chairman Alan Sugar (far left) was about to engage in a vicious split with Venables, while Gascoigne was shortly to be sold to Lazio to assuage yet more off-field financial problems. Tony Berry (far right) would soon leave the board.

1990 Tottenham finish third in Division One
1990 Rumours begin to seep out that severe
debts incurred through the rebuilding of the
East Stand and the failure of various commercial
ventures may force the club into bankruptcy **1991**
Spurs beat Arsenal in the first FA Cup semi-
final to be played at Wembley **1991** Tottenham
win the FA Cup for a record eighth time **1991**
Beating Robert Maxwell to the deal, Alan Sugar
takes over the club; Venables moves "upstairs"
becoming chief executive **1991** Peter Shreeve
returns for his second spell as manager, emulating
Peter McWilliam **1992** Doug Livermore assumes
responsibilities for the first team while reporting
to Venables **1992** The BSkyB TV deal is signed
and First Division teams break away to form the
Premier League **1992** Recovered from injury,
Gascoigne finally completes his move to Lazio
for £5.5m **1993** Sugar and Venables split; the
dispute is eventually taken to the High Court
1993 Ossie Ardiles returns to the club as manager
1993 Tottenham are fined £600,000, banned from
the FA Cup and docked 12 points for financial
malpractice and irregularities during the 1980s; on
appeal the fine is increased but the deduction and
ban rescinded **1994** Jürgen Klinsmann is signed
for $3.3m **1994** After just 18 months in the job
Ardiles is sacked; Gerry Francis takes over

His face contorted with agony, Paul Gascoigne lies injured, his FA Cup final over, and so, too, is his Tottenham career. The midfielder damaged his knee in a reckless tackle on Nottingham Forest's Gary Charles, 18th May 1991.

" *Tyneside's very own renaissance man.*
A man capable of breaking both leg and
wind at the same time.

Jimmy Greaves, on Paul Gascoigne "

Right: Gascoigne and Lineker celebrate a famous win over deadly rivals, after beating Arsenal 3-1 in the 1991 FA Cup semi-final. Gascoigne gave Spurs the lead with one of the greatest ever free-kick goals, before a goal in each half from Lineker sealed the win. The symbolism was acute: Gascoigne and Lineker were rare rays of sunshine in an otherwise dispiriting decade for the club.

Below: A century-old north London scene: Tottenham Hotspur bring the FA Cup back home.

JOE B___ JEANS

Congratulations to:

**TOTTENHAM HOTSPUR
1991
FA CUP WINNERS**

904

–LEGENDS–

Paul Gascoigne

Paul Gascoigne is often held up as the archetypal modern celebrity footballer – the superstar who burst upon the scene to help the country fall in love with the sport again before he became a fixture on the front pages as much as the back. That is only part of the story – famous footballers have always been news but few have generated more column inches than the magnificent, often troubled Geordie genius.

His personal problems have been well documented, but looking back on a topsy-turvy career that took in a number of clubs at home and abroad, there is a convincing case to be made that he played his best football for Spurs. From the moment he arrived at White Hart Lane he was worshipped by the fans, who loved him for his antics as much as his performances. He once scored against Arsenal with a bootless right foot having lost his footwear in a tackle seconds earlier, narrowly escaped serious injury after falling from the East Stand roof while shooting pigeons, and almost single-handedly propelled Tottenham towards the 1991 FA Cup final, notably with a match-winning display in the epic semi-final against Arsenal at Wembley. An ebullient, unpredictable, madcap character, Gazza could infuriate as much as he enthralled, but one thing was for certain: while he was wearing the famous white shirt, no one to witness it could take their eyes off him.

Gazza formed a brief, but productive partnership with Chris Waddle. The regret that these two wonderfully talented footballers could not play together for longer is still lamented by Spurs fans today.

Princess Diana on the receiving end of the unique Gascoigne charm.

FOOTBALL –STATS–

Paul Gascoigne

Name: Paul John Gascoigne

Born: 1967

Playing Career: 1985-2002

Clubs: Newcastle United, Tottenham Hotspur, SS Lazio, Rangers, Middlesbrough, Everton, Burnley

Tottenham Appearances: 110

Goals: 33

–LEGENDS–

Gary Mabbutt

An unwritten rule of modern football dictates that the one-club player is a dying breed. In the age of superagents, transfer merry-go-rounds and the concentration of talent at a dwindling number of Champions League "megabrands", great players tend not to stay too long at clubs that don't consistently challenge for the major honours. Gary Mabbutt doesn't quite fit in to the "one-club legend" category: for one, Spurs was not his first and only team; and secondly, his early Tottenham career coincided with a trophy-winning spell for the club. But in the long years of his subsequent service, punctuated by a single FA Cup win, 'Mabbsie' was Tottenham through and through, and passed up the opportunity to move elsewhere while conducting himself as a role model admired throughout the game.

Mabbutt famously overcame diabetes and confounded those who said the condition would prevent him having a professional career, going on to win 16 England caps. Like his predecessor as skipper Steve Perryman, Mabbutt changed positions, switching from an all-purpose midfield role to become the steadying and inspirational presence at the heart of central defence.

There will no doubt be future players who will earn the distinction of being called a Tottenham legend but for now, Mabbutt ranks as the last of a kind.

FOOTBALL –STATS–

Gary Mabbutt

Name: Gary Vincent Mabbutt MBE

Born: 1961

Playing Career: 1979-1998

Clubs: Bristol Rovers, Tottenham Hotspur

Tottenham Appearances: 586

Goals: 38

Not his prettiest picture, but one that illustrates the extent to which Mabbutt put his body on the line for the Spurs cause. The shattered cheekbone, broken eye socket and shiner was a result of a 'challenge' from Wimbledon's John Fashanu in 1993.

Perhaps the most unsavoury episode for Spurs during the 1990s was the very public and protracted dispute between Alan Sugar and Terry Venables in 1993, which dragged the proud Tottenham name through the gutter. It was symbolic of the off-the-field turmoil (usually centring on money) that has plagued Tottenham – and perhaps football as a whole – in the modern era.

Above: Sugar arrives at the High Court, surrounded by a line of police. The advert on the bus provides a timely and apt backdrop.

Main Picture: Supporters of Venables protest outside the mansion of chairman Alan Sugar in Chigwell, in May 1993.

> *I feel like the guy who shot Bambi.*
> Alan Sugar on sacking Terry Venables

For Jo, Ellen, Carla and Ruby, for putting up with all that Tottenham stuff yet again.

The author would like to thank:

Richard Havers, for his guidance, enthusiasm, knowledge, suggestions, and appreciation of the Spurs way; Paul Moreton and Catherine Bell for the opportunity and generous support; David Scripps, Manjit and the team at Mirrorpix, for their invaluable assistance and patience; all at Haynes publishing and Green Umbrella Publishing.

Special thanks again to Steve Perryman.

To Martin Cloake, a big thanks for his professional expertise and valued friendship, and to Jim and Toby at VSP for their understanding and support.

Thanks also to Bob Goodwin, Phil Soar, Jim Duggan, Andy Porter and others too numerous to mention for sources of information, inspiration and confirmation.

Lastly, utmost respect and gratitude to Frank McGhee, Harry Miller, Monte Fresco, Kent Gavin and the generations of Mirrormen and women who have written about and photographed north London's finest.